W9-ATY-427

Rod and Staff Books

(Milestone Ministries)

800-761-0234 or 541-466-3231

www.RodandStaffBooks.com

Bible Nurture and Reader Series

From a child thou hast known
The HOLY SCRIPTURES
which are able to make
thee wise unto salvation.

Bible Nurture and Reader Series

Exploring with God

Grade 4

Rod and Staff Publishers, Inc.
P.O. Box 3, Hwy. 172
Crockett, Kentucky 41413
Telephone (606) 522-4348

BIBLE NURTURE AND READER SERIES

"If you train your children carefully until they are seven years old, they are already three-quarters educated." This quote recognizes the importance of the critical early years in molding a child's life. The influences of childhood become powerful, lasting impressions.

The type of schoolbooks used certainly affects the developing appetites of our children for reading material. We will not instill in them appreciation for godly values by feeding them frivolous nonsense. We hold the Bible to be the highest guide for life and the best source of training for our children. The Bible reveals God and His will. Proverbs 9:10 says, "The fear of the Lord is the beginning of wisdom: and the knowledge of the holy is understanding." It is important that our children are exposed to truth from the beginning of their learning experience.

For the student to be exposed to the truth of God's Word only in textbooks is not sufficient to give him the very best. It is necessary for the tutor, be he parent or other teacher, to be firmly rooted in the Word of God and have the power of God's presence in his life. The Bible must be treasured as God's message to mankind. On that conviction this series is built, with the Scriptures as its very substance.

This book is designed as part of a series and will be most effective if so used. The grade four material includes the following books.

Teacher's Manual	Reading Workbook Unit 1
	Reading Workbook Unit 2
Pupil's Reader	Reading Workbook Unit 3

Copyright, 1988

First edition, copyright 1966; revisions 1969, 1988

By
Rod and Staff Publishers, Inc.
Crockett, Kentucky 41413

Printed in U.S.A.

ISBN 0-7399-0394-2

Catalog no. 11401.3

12   13   14   15   16   —   19   18   17   16   15   14   13   12   11   10

Table of Contents

Unit 1

The Gospel of John

Unit 2

The Book of Acts

Unit 3

Job, Psalms, Proverbs

Unit One

The Gospel of John

Introduction to John

The stories in this unit are from the Gospel of John, the fourth book of the New Testament. There are four Johns mentioned in the New Testament. The first one is John the Baptist, the son of Zacharias the priest. The second John is the son of Zebedee and brother of James. In the Book of Acts, we find the other two Johns. One is a disciple known as John Mark. The other one, a relative of the high priest, was not a disciple of Jesus.

It was John, the brother of James, who wrote the Gospel according to John. He is the only John who was one of the twelve apostles. He was called the beloved disciple because he was a close friend of Jesus. He seemed well able to understand much of the truth that Jesus taught. Because he followed the Lord closely, John could write well the things Jesus did and taught while He was here on the earth. The Holy Spirit brought these things to his memory after Jesus went back to heaven, and He gave him the words to write. The Gospel according to John is one of the best-loved books of the Bible.

Jesus Comes to Earth

John 1:1–18

We usually think of a person's beginning as the day he was born, but this was not true of Jesus. He always was with God. He was with God when the world was created. John tells us, "All things were made by him."

Before Jesus was born into the world, John the Baptist was sent by God to prepare the way for Jesus. John was to tell the people when He came. Jesus made the world and the people in the world. Yet the people did not even know the One who made both them and the world in which they were living.

The Jews were God's chosen people. They had been chosen to write the Bible and bring the knowledge of God to others. Jesus was born into a Jewish home, but many of His own Jewish people would not receive Him. They turned away from the One who made them and the world in which they lived. They hated the loving One who came to save them from their sins and take them to a better home. Truly Jesus came into a very wicked world and to a proud, unthankful people.

Yet Jesus had a heart of love for sinful people. To all people who would receive Him, He gave power to become the sons of God. They are God's sons not because they are born into a special human family, but because they believe in Jesus and obey Him.

13

Jesus was given a body of flesh when He came as a human baby. He lived among men, and His life was full of grace and truth. People who lived at that time saw the glory of the heavenly Father in Jesus' life.

When John the Baptist saw Jesus, he told the people, "This is the One whom I have been telling you about. He is greater than I am, for He was before I was." John had been born before Jesus, but Jesus had lived long before John's birth. Jesus was in the beginning with God.

John the Baptist Reveals Jesus
John 1:19–51

The Jewish people had the Scriptures, and they knew the prophecies that someday Jesus would come into the world. For many, many years they had been waiting and looking for Him to come.

Now when John the Baptist came preaching and baptizing, they thought perhaps he was the Christ for whom they were looking. The Jewish leaders sent priests and Levites from Jerusalem to John the Baptist, who was baptizing people on the other side of the Jordan River. These men came to John and asked, "Who are you?"

John answered, "I am not the Christ."

"Then who are you?" they inquired. "Are you Elijah?"

John assured them, "I am not."

"Are you that prophet?" they questioned.

"No," replied John.

Now the priests and Levites knew who John was not, but they still did not know who he was. So they asked, "Who are you, that we may give an answer to those who sent us? What do you say about yourself?"

John said, "I am the voice of one crying in the

wilderness, 'Make straight the way of the Lord,' as the prophet Isaiah said."

John did not think of himself as being anyone great. He called himself only a voice. He had come as a voice to tell the people about Jesus, the Great One.

The priests and Levites asked, "Why then do you baptize, if you are not the Christ, nor Elijah, neither that prophet?"

John answered, "I baptize with water, but there is One standing among you whom you do not know. He is the One who is coming after me, but is preferred before me. I am not worthy to loosen His shoestrings."

The next day John saw Jesus coming to him. "Behold the Lamb of God, who takes away the sin of the world!" said John. "This is the One I was telling you about when I said, 'After me comes a Man who is preferred before me, for He was before me.' I would not have known who He is, except that He should be made known to Israel. That is why I came baptizing with water."

John did not know of himself that this was Jesus. But God had revealed it to him so that he could tell others. God had told John that the One on whom he saw the Spirit come down and remain, He it was who would baptize with the Holy Spirit. And John saw the Spirit descend from heaven like a dove and rest upon Jesus. So John knew that this was God's Son, for whom he had been sent to prepare the way.

The next day when John was standing with two of

his followers, he again saw Jesus walking. "Behold the Lamb of God!" he said to them.

When the two followers of John heard this, they began following Jesus. Jesus turned and saw that they were following Him. He asked them, "What are you seeking?"

They said to Him, "Master where do You dwell?"

"Come and see," Jesus invited.

They came and saw where He dwelled and stayed with him that day because it was about four o'clock in the afternoon.

One of the two men who followed Jesus was Andrew, the brother of Simon Peter. He went to find Peter, saying, "We have found the Christ." Andrew brought Peter to Jesus.

When Jesus saw Peter, He said, "You are Simon the son of Jona. You shall be called Cephas, which means 'a stone.' "

The next day Jesus wanted to go into Galilee. He found Philip and said to him, "Follow Me." Philip lived in Bethsaida, the same city in which Peter and Andrew lived. It was a city just north of the Sea of Galilee and next to the country of Galilee.

Philip, like Andrew, wanted to share the good news of finding Jesus. He found Nathanael and said to him, "We have found the One about whom Moses and the prophets wrote—Jesus of Nazareth, the Son of Joseph."

But Nazareth was such an unimportant place that Nathanael doubted whether the Promised One would come from there. He asked Philip, "Can any good thing come out of Nazareth?"

"Come and see," invited Philip.

When Jesus saw Nathanael coming to Him, He said, "Here is a true Israelite. There is no deceit in him." (Many Israelites were deceitful. They pretended to be righteous but were not.)

Nathanael was surprised that Jesus knew him. He said, "How do You know me?"

Jesus answered, "Before Philip called you, when you were under the fig tree, I saw you."

Nathanael said, "Master, You are the Son of God. You are the King of Israel."

Jesus asked, "Do you believe because I said I saw you under a fig tree? You will see greater things than these. After this you shall see heaven open and the angels of God ascending and descending upon the Son of Man.'"

The Beginning of Jesus' Ministry
John 2

On the third day there was a marriage in the city of Cana, which was in Galilee. It was the town in which Nathanael lived and was close to Nazareth, Jesus' childhood home.

Mary, the mother of Jesus, was at the wedding, and Jesus and His disciples were also invited.

Wine was served at this wedding, but it was all used up before the wedding was over. Mary came to Jesus and said, "They have no wine." Then she told the servants to do whatever Jesus told them to do.

Nearby were six stone water pots, each of which held about sixteen to twenty-four gallons of water. They were there because the Jews were very particular about washing their hands before they ate. So they needed plenty of water. "Fill the pots with water," said Jesus, and the servants filled them to the brim.

Jesus said, "Draw some out now, and carry it to the ruler of the feast." The servants carried it to the ruler as Jesus had commanded.

When the ruler of the feast tasted it, he was very much surprised. He called the man who had just been married and said, "Everyone serves the good wine first, and when men have had nearly all they want, then they serve that which is worse. But you have kept the good wine until now."

The ruler did not know where this good wine had come from. Only the servants knew it was water that Jesus had turned into wine. The ruler thought that the man who had just gotten married was doing things in an unusual way.

This was the first miracle that Jesus performed. The miracle showed His glory, and His disciples believed on Him.

After this, Jesus, His mother and brothers, and His disciples went to the town of Capernaum and stayed there a few days. It was the time when the Jews kept the Feast of the Passover at Jerusalem, and Jesus wanted to go to this feast. So Jesus went up to Jerusalem and entered the temple.

There Jesus saw something that made Him very sad. In the temple were many people selling sheep, oxen, and doves. The people needed these animals for sacrifices, but the temple was not the place to sell them. Changers of money were also sitting there. They needed to change the money of people from other countries so that those people would have the right kind of money to buy animals. But the temple was not the place to do these things. This was God's house and should have been a house of prayer, not a marketplace.

Jesus made a whip of small cords and drove them all out of the temple, including the sheep and the oxen. He poured out the changers' money and turned over their tables. To those who sold doves He said, "Take these things out of here. Do not make My Father's house a house of buying and selling."

Then Jesus' disciples remembered what is said in the Book of Psalms about this. Jesus had a great zeal to see God's house kept pure and clean.

The Jews could not understand what right Jesus had to come into the temple and do what He had just done. They said, "What sign can You show us to prove that You have the right to do these things?"

When we see a man dressed as a policeman and wearing a badge, we know he has the authority to see that people obey the laws. He has the right to punish them if they do not obey. Other people do not have this right. Now the Jews wanted Jesus to show what authority He had to come into the temple and upset things.

Jesus said to them, "Destroy this temple, and in three days I will raise it up."

To the Jews, this seemed like an impossible thing. They said, "It took forty-six years to build this temple, and will You build it in three days?"

They did not understand that Jesus was talking about the temple of His body. They would crucify Him. He would give His life for their sins, but in three days He would rise again. This would truly be a great sign and another proof that He is the Son of God.

After Jesus rose from the dead, the disciples remembered what Jesus had said at this time. They believed the Scriptures and the words that Jesus had spoken.

While Jesus was in Jerusalem at the Passover, many people believed in Him when they saw the miracles that He did. Jesus knew what was in the hearts of these people without anyone telling Him. He knew whether they were sincere believers or whether they were only deceivers.

Jesus Explains the New Birth

John 3:1-8

One of the rulers of the Jews, Nicodemus, came to Jesus at night. He said to Jesus, "Master, we know that You are a teacher come from God, for no man can do these miracles that You are doing unless God is with him."

Jesus answered Nicodemus, "Verily, verily, I say to you that unless a man is born again, he cannot see the kingdom of God."

This was a new idea to Nicodemus. He did not know what Jesus was talking about. He could not understand how a man could be born again. As far as he knew, people are born only once. But he was thinking only about being born as a human baby. Jesus was thinking of another birth, by which a man becomes a son of God through believing in Jesus. He was speaking of being born of the Spirit of God and having fellowship with God.

Nicodemus was a Pharisee. The Pharisees were Jews who claimed to believe and obey the Scriptures. Yet Nicodemus did not even know how to enter into the kingdom of God. He was trying to teach other people the way to heaven and did not know the way himself.

Nicodemus asked Jesus, "How can a man be born when he is old?"

Jesus answered, "Verily, verily, I say to you, that unless a man is born of water and of the Spirit, he cannot enter into the kingdom of God."

Jesus went on to explain to Nicodemus the difference between being born the first time and being born the second time. The first birth is of earthly parents and gives us a body of flesh. We are made with the nature of our parents. The second birth is of the Spirit of God, which gives a man the nature of God.

Jesus said, "Do not be astonished that I said to you, 'You must be born again.' The wind blows where it wants to blow. You hear the sound of it, but you cannot tell where it comes from or where it goes. That is the way it is with everyone who is born of the Spirit."

Nicodemus still could not understand what Jesus was trying to tell him. He asked, "How can these things be?"

Jesus answered, "Are you a teacher of Israel and do not know these things? Verily, verily, I say to you that we talk about things we know and tell about the things we have seen, and you do not receive it. If I have told you earthly things and you do not believe, how shall you believe if I tell you heavenly things?"

Then Jesus told Nicodemus more about God's marvelous plan of salvation. He said, "As Moses lifted up the serpent in the wilderness, even so must the Son of Man be lifted up, so that whoever believes in Him should not perish but have eternal life. For God so loved the world, that He gave His only begotten Son, so that whoever believes in Him should not perish but have everlasting life."

Perhaps you remember the story of Moses lifting up the serpent in the wilderness. The children of Israel were traveling, and the way was becoming hard and long. They were greatly discouraged and began to find fault with God and with Moses for bringing them out of Egypt into the wilderness.

The Lord was displeased with them for complaining. He sent fiery serpents among the people. They bit the people and many of them died.

The people who were still alive became frightened. They came to Moses and said, "We have sinned, for we have spoken against the Lord and against you. Pray to the Lord that He will take away the serpents from us."

Moses prayed for the people. The Lord said to Moses, "Make a fiery serpent and set it upon a pole. Then it shall be that everyone who is bitten, when he looks at it, shall live."

Moses made a serpent of brass and put it upon a pole. And it was so, that if a serpent had bitten any of the people and that person looked at the serpent of brass, he lived.

This story helps us to understand the beautiful story of salvation. All mankind has been bitten by the terrible serpent of sin. So everyone will die and be separated from God forever unless Someone gives help. Jesus took upon Himself the sins of all the world when He was lifted up on the cross to die. Now everyone who trusts in Him will be saved and have eternal life.

Jesus and the Woman at the Well
John 4:1–42

For a while Jesus and His disciples were baptizing people in the land of Judea. Jesus Himself did not baptize people, but His disciples did. Then Jesus left Judea to go into Galilee. To get there, He needed to go through the country of Samaria.

Jesus came to a city in Samaria called Sychar. This was near the piece of ground that Jacob had given to his son Joseph. Jacob's well was at Sychar, and because Jesus was weary from traveling, He sat down at the well. It was about noon, and the disciples went into the city to buy something to eat.

A woman of Samaria came to the well to draw water. Jesus said, "Please give Me a drink."

The woman recognized that Jesus was a Jew, and she was very much surprised that Jesus would ask her for a drink. The Jews disliked the Samaritans and did not want to have any dealings with them. She asked Jesus, "How is it that You, being a Jew, ask for a drink from me, a woman of Samaria?"

Jesus said to her, "If you knew the gift of God and who it is that says to you, 'Give Me a drink,' you would have asked Him, and He would have given you living

water."

The woman said to Him, "Sir, You have nothing to draw with, and the well is deep. From where then do You have that living water? Are You greater than our father Jacob, who gave us the well, and drank of it himself, and his children, and his livestock?"

Jesus answered, "Whoever drinks of this water shall get thirsty again, but whoever drinks of the water that I give him shall never thirst. The water that I give him shall be in him a well of water springing up into everlasting life."

What wonderful words! The woman wanted this water so that she could drink and not get thirsty again. She said to Jesus, "Sir, give me this water so that I will not become thirsty and do not need to come here to draw water."

Jesus said to her, "Go, call your husband and come here."

The woman said to Jesus, "I have no husband."

Jesus said, "You have well said, 'I have no husband.' For you have had five husbands, and the man you now have is not your husband. In this you spoke truly."

This woman was getting many surprises. How did Jesus know so much about her? She said, "Sir, I can see that You are a prophet. Our fathers worshiped in this mountain, and you [Jews] say that in Jerusalem is the place where men ought to worship."

Jesus said to her, "Woman, believe Me, the hour is coming when you shall neither worship the Father in this mountain, nor yet at Jerusalem. You do not know what you worship. We know what we worship, for salvation is of the Jews. The hour is coming, and now is, when the true worshipers shall worship the Father in spirit and in truth, for the Father is looking for such people to worship Him. God is a Spirit, and they who worship Him must worship Him in spirit and in truth."

The woman said to Him, "I know that Messiah who is called Christ is coming. When He comes, He will tell us all things."

Jesus said to her, "I that speak to you am He."

Just then the disciples came back. They were surprised that Jesus was talking with this woman of Samaria, yet none of them asked Jesus what He was seeking or why He talked with her.

The woman then left her water pot and went back into the city. She said to the men, "Come, see a Man who told me everything that I ever did. Is not this the Christ?" The men went out of the city and came to Jesus.

In the meantime, while the woman was gone, Jesus' disciples asked Him to eat. But Jesus said, "I have food to eat that you do not know about."

The disciples questioned among themselves, "Has anyone brought Him anything to eat?"

Jesus said, "My food is to do the will of Him who sent Me and to finish His work. Do you not say, 'There are yet four months, and then harvest comes'? Behold, I say to you, lift up your eyes and look on the fields; for they are white already to harvest."

Jesus had His eyes on things more important than the harvesting of crops. He was thinking of people as being the harvest. He meant that it was time for them to hear the Gospel so that they could believe and be saved.

Many of the Samaritans of the city believed in Jesus because of the words that the woman said about Him when she said, "He told me everything that I ever did."

After the Samaritans had come to Jesus, they begged Him to stay with them. So He stayed there two days. Many more believed in Him during this time. They said to the woman, "Now we believe, not because of what you said, but because we have heard Him ourselves. We know that this is indeed the Christ, the Saviour of the world."

Jesus Performs Miracles of Healing

John 4:43–5:18

After staying two days in Samaria, Jesus went on His way again into Galilee. The people in Galilee received Him because they had also gone to the feast at Jerusalem and had seen Jesus' miracles there.

Jesus came again into Cana, where He had made the water into wine. Over at Capernaum, a town not far from Cana, there was a nobleman who had a son that was very sick. He was so sick that he was about to die. When the nobleman heard that Jesus had returned from Judea into Galilee, he went to Jesus and begged Him to come down and heal his son.

Jesus said to him, "Unless you see signs and wonders, you will not believe."

The man was anxious for Jesus to come and help him quickly. He said to Jesus, "Sir, come down before my child dies."

Jesus said to him, "Go your way. Your son lives."

The man believed the word that Jesus had spoken to him and went his way. As he was going, his servants met him and told him, "Your son lives."

The father inquired from them at what time his son began to get better. They said, "Yesterday at one o'clock in the afternoon, the fever left him."

The father knew that this was the same hour that Jesus had said to him, "Your son lives." The nobleman and all the people in the house believed in Jesus because of this.

Soon afterward there was a feast of the Jews, and Jesus again went up to Jerusalem.

At Jerusalem by the sheep market there was a pool that had five porches around it. In these porches many sick people were lying. Some of them were blind. Some were lame. All of them were waiting for the moving of the water. At certain times an angel would go down into the pool and trouble the water. The first person who stepped into the water after this stirring was healed of whatever disease he had.

A certain man was there who had been sick thirty-eight years. Jesus saw him lying there and knew that he had been in that condition a long time. He said to the man, "Would you like to be made well?"

The man answered Him, "Sir, I have no one, when the water is troubled, to put me into the pool. But while I am coming, another one steps in ahead of me."

Jesus said to him, "Arise, take up your bed, and walk."

Immediately the man became well. He took up his bed and began walking.

It was the Sabbath Day when this man was made well. The Jews found fault with the man because he was carrying his bed on the Sabbath Day. They said to him,

"It is not lawful for you to carry your bed."

He answered, "The One who made me well said to me, 'Take up your bed and walk.'"

They asked him, "Who said to you, 'Take up your bed and walk'?"

But the man did not know who it was that had healed him because many people were there, and Jesus had gone away.

Later Jesus found the man in the temple and said to him, "See, you are well. Do not sin any more, lest a worse thing come upon you."

The man left and told the Jews that it was Jesus who had made him well.

Because Jesus had done these things on the Sabbath Day, the Jews persecuted Him and tried to find a way to kill Him.

Jesus answered them, "My Father works until now, and I work."

This angered the Jews all the more. Not only had Jesus broken their Sabbath rules, but He had spoken of God as His Father, making Himself equal with God.

Jesus Feeds the Five Thousand
John 6

After these things Jesus went over the Sea of Galilee. Great multitudes of people followed Him because they had seen His miracles of healing for the people who were diseased.

Almost a year had passed since Jesus had gone up to Jerusalem to the Feast of the Passover. It was again nearing the time that this feast was to be held. Jesus went up into a mountain, and there He sat down with His disciples.

When Jesus looked up and saw all the people who had followed Him, He asked Philip, "Where shall we buy bread so that these may have something to eat?" Jesus did not ask this question because the need was any problem to Him. He knew what He would do, but He asked it to see what Philip would say. Did Philip have faith that Jesus could take care of the people?

Philip said to Jesus, "Two hundred pennyworth of bread is not enough that each one of them may have even a little." Two hundred pence was eight months' wages at that time.

Simon Peter's brother Andrew said, "There is a lad here who has five barley loaves and two small fishes.

But what are they among so many?"

Jesus said, "Have the people sit down."

It was a nice grassy place, so all the people sat down. All together there were about five thousand men.

Jesus took the five loaves and gave thanks to God for them. Then He divided the bread and gave it to His disciples, and the disciples passed it out to those who were sitting down. They also gave out as much fish as the people wanted.

When all the people were filled, Jesus said to His disciples, "Gather up the fragments that are left so that nothing is lost."

They gathered the fragments together and filled twelve baskets with them. All this was left after the multitudes had been filled. It was more than they had at the beginning!

When the men saw the miracle that Jesus had done, they said, "This is truly that prophet that should come into the world."

Jesus realized that they thought of Him as a great prophet and that they intended to come and force Him to be their king. So He went off into a mountain to be alone.

In the evening the disciples went down to the sea. They got into a ship and started across the sea toward Capernaum. It became dark, and Jesus was not with them. A great wind began to blow, causing the waves of the sea to become high. The disciples rowed for some distance, and then they saw Jesus walking on the sea and coming near the ship. They were very much afraid, for they did not know that it was Jesus. They could not tell who it was.

Jesus said to them, "It is I. Do not be afraid."

What a great comfort it was when the disciples realized it was Jesus! They willingly received Him into their ship, and immediately they were at the land where they were planning to go.

The people had seen the disciples leave in the only ship there. They knew Jesus had not gone with the disciples, but He was not with the people either. So the next day the people crossed the sea in other boats, and they came to Capernaum, looking for Jesus.

When they found Him on the other side of the sea, they asked Him, "Master, when did You come here?"

Jesus said to them, "You do not look for Me because you saw the miracles, but because you ate of the loaves and were filled. Do not work for the food that passes away, but for that which endures to everlasting life."

They asked Jesus, "What shall we do so that we may work the works of God?"

Jesus answered, "This is the work of God, that you believe in the One whom He has sent."

They asked Him, "What sign do You show us then, so that we might see and believe? What do You work?"

This was a poor question to ask. Jesus had already shown by His power that He was the Son of God. They could have believed if they had wanted to, but they were not willing to believe in Jesus. They needed to recognize themselves as sinners and give up their sins, but they were not willing to do this.

Jesus told them many things about Himself, but they did not understand the things He was trying to tell them. From that time on, many of His followers went away and did not walk with Him anymore.

Jesus asked the twelve, "Will you also go away?"

Peter answered, "Lord, to whom shall we go? You have the words of eternal life. And we believe and are sure that You are that Christ, the Son of the living God."

Jesus said, "Have I not chosen you twelve, and one of you is a devil?" He was speaking about Judas, the son of Simon because He knew that he was the one who would betray Him.

The Pharisees Seek Jesus' Life

John 7

After this, Jesus spent most of His time in Galilee because in Judea the Jews were looking for an opportunity to kill Him.

The time came for the Jews to keep a feast called the Feast of Tabernacles. Jesus' brothers said to Him, "Leave here, and go into Judea so that Your disciples may also see the works that You are doing. For no man does anything in secret. He wants others to know what he is doing. If You do these things, show Yourself to the world."

These words could make it sound as if Jesus' brothers believed in Him, and wanted others to see Jesus' miracles so that they would also believe. But that was not true. Jesus' brothers still did not believe that Jesus was the Son of God. They thought that if He truly did what it seemed He could do, He should not hesitate to go to Judea and show His followers there what He could do.

But Jesus knew what might happen if He went to Jerusalem right away. He was willing to die for the sins of the people when the time came, but it was not yet that time. He said to His brothers, "My time has not yet come, but your time is always ready. The world cannot hate you, but it hates Me because I tell them about the evil of the things they are doing. You go up to this feast. I will not go now because My hour is not yet come."

So Jesus' brothers went up to the feast without Him, and Jesus stayed a little longer in Galilee. Then He also went to the feast, but He went secretly. He did not want people to know where He was just then.

The Jews were expecting Jesus to come to the feast, and they looked for Him there. They asked, "Where is He?"

Much discussion was going on about Jesus. The people had many different opinions about who He was. Some of them said, "He is a good Man." Others said, "No, but He deceives the people." They were very careful, however, to whom they told their opinions because they were afraid of the Jewish leaders.

When the feast was about half over, Jesus went into the temple. There He taught the people as He had done before.

These people were astonished at the way Jesus could teach. They asked, "How does this Man know letters without ever having learned?" There was no question about Jesus' ability to read and teach. But the people did not know how He could do it because He had never gone to the schools of Jerusalem's priests and scribes. If they had believed that He is God and knows all things, they would not have needed to be perplexed about so many things.

Jesus said, "My teaching is not Mine, but it comes from the One who sent Me. If anyone wants to do the will of God, He will know whether My teaching is from God, or whether I speak of myself."

Jesus asked them, "Did not Moses give you the Law, and yet none of you keeps the Law? Why do you go about to kill me?"

The people answered, "You have a devil. Who is going about to kill You?" This was a terrible thing to say about Jesus, but He continued to teach them and try to help them.

Some of the people at Jerusalem asked, "Is this not the Man whom they are seeking to kill? But look, He is speaking boldly, and they do not say anything to Him. Do the rulers know for sure that this is the very Christ?"

Then as Jesus was teaching in the temple, He said, "You both know Me, and you know where I am from. I have not come of Myself, but He that sent Me is true, whom you do not know. But I know Him, for I am from Him and He has sent Me."

After He had said these things, the Jews tried to take Him. But no one was able to do it because the time had not yet come that Jesus should die.

There were many people who believed in Jesus. They said, "When Christ comes, will He do more miracles than these which this Man has done?" They did not think so. They thought the things Jesus did were proof enough that He was Christ.

The Pharisees heard that the people were saying

these things about Jesus, and they did not like it. They wanted to get rid of Him before more people believed in Him. The Pharisees and the chief priests sent officers to go and take Jesus.

Jesus told the people, "For a little while longer I am with you, and then I will go to Him who sent Me." And on the last day of the feast, He stood up and cried out, "If anyone is thirsty, let him come to Me and drink." Whoever believes in Jesus will receive many blessings, and he will be a blessing to many other people.

Some of the people thought Jesus was the prophet who was to come into the world. Some said, "This is the Christ." But others thought this could hardly be. "Shall Christ come out of Galilee?" they asked. "Does not the Scripture say that Christ comes of the seed of David and out of the town of Bethlehem, where David was?" So the people were not agreed about Jesus. Some of them wanted to kill Him, but no one laid hands on Him at this time.

The officers who had been sent to take Jesus came back to the chief priests and Pharisees.

They asked, "Why have you not brought Him?"

The officers answered, "No man ever spoke like this Man."

The Pharisees asked, "Are you also deceived? Have any of the rulers or any of the Pharisees believed in Him?"

Nicodemus, who had come to Jesus by night, was in the group. He asked, "Does our Law judge any man before listening to him and knowing what he does?"

They answered, "Are you also from Galilee? Search and look, for out of Galilee comes no prophet."

Every man went to his own house.

Guilty Accusers

John 8

Jesus went to the Mount of Olives, and early in the morning He came again into the temple. All the people came to Him, and He sat down and taught them.

Then the scribes and Pharisees brought to Jesus a woman who had broken the seventh commandment. That commandment says, "Thou shalt not commit adultery."

They brought the woman in and put her in the midst. Then they said, "Master, this woman was taken in the very act of adultery. Now Moses in the Law commanded us that such should be stoned. But what do You say?"

They asked this to tempt Jesus so that they could find fault with Him. They did not bring this sinful woman to Him because they hated sin. Their own lives were sinful, too. They were very eager to keep the things in the Law of Moses that made them appear good to others. But they were hypocrites and only pretended to be good. They wanted to cover their own sins, and they looked down on people who were known to be sinners.

Jesus did not answer their question. He stooped down, and with His finger He began writing on the ground. But when they continued to ask Him, He lifted

Himself up and said to them, "He who does not have any sin among you, let him be the first one to cast a stone at her."

Jesus again stooped down and wrote on the ground.

The men's consciences began to bother them. They knew they were not without sin. None of them had a right to throw a stone at the woman. They were just as guilty of sin as she. The oldest man among them left. All the other men followed one by one.

Finally Jesus was left alone with the woman standing in the midst. When Jesus lifted Himself up again, He did not see anyone but the woman nearby. He asked her, "Woman, where are your accusers? Has no man condemned you?"

The woman answered, "No man, Lord."

Jesus said to her, "Neither do I condemn you. Go, and sin no more."

After this Jesus again taught in the temple, but the Jews could not understand the things He was trying to tell them. One time He said, "I go My way, and you shall look for Me but shall die in your sins. Where I go, you cannot come."

They could not understand where Jesus was going that they could not come. "Will He kill Himself?" they wondered. "Where is He going?"

Another time He said to the Jews who believed on Him, "If you continue in My Word, then you are My disciples indeed. And you shall know the truth, and the truth shall make you free."

The Jews did not understand this. They said, "We are not in bondage. We are descendants of Abraham." They did not realize that they were bound by sin. Some of them were so sinful that they wanted to kill the Son of God.

Jesus said, "Verily, verily, I say to you, that if a man keeps My saying, He shall never see death."

To the unbelieving Jews this seemed like a terrible lie. They said, "Now we know that You have a devil. Abraham and the prophets are dead. Yet You say, 'If a man keeps My saying, he shall never taste of death.' Are You greater than our father Abraham, who is dead? The prophets are dead also. Whom do You make Yourself?"

They thought surely Abraham and the prophets had kept God's Word, and yet they had died. How could this saying of Jesus be true?

Jesus did not mean that the body would not die. The body is not really the person. It is only the house in which the person lives. All who keep the Word of the Lord will live with Him forever and will never see death. Abraham and the prophets were alive. Their souls had gone to be with God. Jesus said, "Your father Abraham rejoiced to see My day, and he saw it and was glad."

Now this saying seemed more ridiculous than ever to the Jews. Abraham had lived on the earth nearly two thousand years before this time and had died long before Jesus was born. How could Abraham see the time when Jesus would come? They said to Jesus, "You are not yet fifty years old, and have You seen Abraham?"

Jesus answered them. "Verily, verily, I say to you that before Abraham was, I am."

The angry Jews took up stones to throw at Jesus. But Jesus hid himself and went out of the temple, going right through the midst of them, and passed by.

Sight and Salvation for a Blind Man

John 9:1–38

As Jesus was passing by, He saw a man who was blind from the time that he was born.

The disciples asked, "Master, who sinned, this man or his parents, that he was born blind?"

Jesus said, "This man was not born blind because of his parents' sins or because of his own sins, but so that the works of God might be shown in him. I must work the works of God while it is daytime, because the night comes when no man can work. As long as I am in the world, I am the light of the world."

When Jesus had said this, He spit upon the ground and made clay of it. Then He anointed the eyes of the blind man with the clay and said, "Go, wash in the pool of Siloam."

The blind man went his way and washed as Jesus had told him. When he came back, he could see!

The neighbors and other people who had seen the blind man before were curious about what had happened. They said, "Is not this the one who sat and begged?"

Some said, "This is he."

Others said, "He is like him."

The man who had been blind said, "I am he."

So they asked him, "How were your eyes opened?"

The man answered, "A man who is called Jesus made clay and anointed my eyes and said to me, 'Go to the pool of Siloam and wash.' I went and washed and received sight."

They asked him, "Where is He?"

"I do not know," said the man who had just received his sight.

They brought the man to the Pharisees to see what they would say about what had happened. It was on the Sabbath Day that Jesus had made the clay and opened the man's eyes.

The Pharisees asked the man how he had received his sight.

The man said, "He put clay upon my eyes, and I washed and do see."

Some of the Pharisees said about Jesus, "This Man is not of God, because He does not keep the Sabbath Day."

Others said, "How can a man who is a sinner do such miracles?" So there was a great difference of opinion among them.

They asked the blind man, "What do you say about Him who has opened your eyes?"

He answered, "He is a prophet."

But the Jews did not believe that this was the same man who had been blind. They were not satisfied to take his word for it until they had called his parents.

They asked the parents, "Is this your son, whom you say was born blind? How then does he see?"

The parents answered, "We know that this is our son and that he was born blind. But by what means he now sees we do not know, or who has opened his eyes we do not know. He is of age; ask him. He shall speak for himself."

The parents said this because they were afraid of the Jews. The Jews had already agreed that anyone who said he believed in Jesus would be put out of the synagogue. For this reason the parents said, "He is of age; ask him."

Again the Jews called in the man who had been blind. "Give God the praise," they said. "We know that this Man is a sinner."

The man answered, "Whether He is a sinner or not, I do not know. One thing I know, that whereas I was blind, now I can see."

Again they asked him, "What did He do to you? How did He open your eyes?"

He answered them, "I have told you already, and you did not listen. Why do you want to hear it again? Will you also be His disciples?"

Then they began to revile him. They said, "You are His disciple, but we are Moses' disciples. We know that God spoke to Moses. As for this fellow, we do not know where He is from."

The man answered, "Why, here is a marvelous thing, that you do not know where He is from, and yet He has opened my eyes. Now we know that God does not hear sinners; but if any man be a worshiper of God and does His will, him God hears.

"Since the world began, no one has ever heard of anyone opening the eyes of one who was born blind. If this Man were not of God, He could do nothing."

The Pharisees answered, "You were altogether born in sins, and do you teach us?" Then they cast him out of the synagogue.

Jesus heard that they had cast him out. When Jesus found him He said, "Do you believe on the Son of God?"

The man answered, "Who is He, Lord, that I might believe on Him?"

Jesus said to him, "You have both seen Him, and it is He who is talking with you."

"Lord, I believe," said the man. And he worshiped Him.

The Good Shepherd

John 10

Jesus often told stories to help people understand some truth that He wanted to teach them. One time He told about how things are in a sheepfold (a pen for sheep). He said, "Verily, Verily, I say to you, if someone does not enter by the door into the sheepfold, but climbs up some other way, he is a thief and a robber. But when a shepherd comes to the sheepfold, he enters by the door."

A porter, or doorkeeper, stands at the door to guard it. If thieves or robbers come to the sheepfold, they try to get in by climbing over the high fence or wall. They know the porter will not open the door for them. But when the shepherd comes to the door, the porter lets him in because the shepherd is a good man and will not harm the sheep. The sheep rejoice to know that their shepherd is there.

Jesus said, "The porter opens the door for the shepherd, and the sheep hear his voice. The shepherd calls each sheep by name and leads them out. Then he walks before them, and the sheep follow him because they know his voice. If a stranger calls to them, they will not follow him because they do not recognize his voice."

The people who heard this story did not understand what Jesus was trying to teach them. He said, "Verily, verily, I say to you, I am the Door of the sheep. All who ever came before Me are thieves and robbers, but the sheep did not listen to them. I am the Door. If any man enters in by Me, he shall be saved and shall go in and out and find pasture.

"The thief does not come except to steal and to kill and to destroy. I have come that people might have life and that they might have it more abundantly. I am the Good Shepherd. The Good Shepherd gives His life for the sheep."

Sometimes a hireling (hired worker) watches over the sheep. Jesus said, "When a hireling sees a wolf coming, he leaves the sheep and runs away to save his life. He does this because he is a hireling and does not care about the sheep.

"I have other sheep, which are not of this fold. I must also bring them in, and there shall be one fold and one Shepherd." The sheep of the fold were God's chosen people, the Jews. The other sheep were the Gentiles. But God loves all people, and through Jesus He wants everyone to come into His fold.

Jesus said, "My Father loves Me because I lay down My life for the sheep. No man takes it from Me, but I lay it down of Myself. I have power to lay it down, and I have power to take it again." After Jesus gave His life, He would rise and live forever.

When Jesus said these things, the Jews again had different opinions about Him. Some said, "He has a devil and is out of His mind. Why do you listen to Him?"

Others said, "These are not the words of someone who has a devil. Can a devil open the eyes of the blind?" These things took place at Jerusalem during the Jews' Feast of Dedication, when it was wintertime.

Later Jesus was walking in the temple in Solomon's porch. The Jews came to Him and said, "How long do You make us doubt? If You are the Christ, tell us plainly."

Jesus said, "I told you, and you did not believe. The works that I do in My father's Name, they speak for Me. But you do not believe because you are not of My sheep, as I told you before. My sheep hear My voice, and I know them, and they follow Me. I give them eternal life and they shall never perish, neither shall any man pluck them out of My hand. I and My Father are one."

These words angered the Jews, and they picked up stones to stone Him.

Jesus said, "I have showed you many good works. For which of those do you stone Me?"

They answered, "We do not stone You for a good work, but for blasphemy; because You, being a Man, make Yourself God."

Jesus said, "If I am not doing the works of My Father, do not believe Me. But if I am, even though you do not believe Me, believe the works that I do. Then you will know that the Father is in Me and I am in Him."

This made the Jews all the more angry. They tried to arrest Jesus, but He escaped out of their hands and went to the other side of the Jordan where John at first had baptized. There He stayed for a while.

Many people came to Jesus and believed on Him there. They believed because everything that John had said about Jesus was true, and also because Jesus had done many miracles. John had done no miracles, but all the things he had said about Jesus were right.

A Death for the Glory of God

John 11:1–45

In the small town of Bethany, which was not very far from Jerusalem, there lived a man and his two sisters. Their names were Lazarus and Mary and Martha. Jesus loved these people very much.

Lazarus became sick. His sisters sent word to Jesus, saying, "Lord, behold, the one whom You love is sick."

When Jesus heard this message, He said, "This sickness is not to death. Rather, it is for the glory of God, so that the Son of God might be glorified from it."

Jesus did not rush to their house right away to see what He could do for Lazarus. He stayed two more days in the place where He was. Then He said to the disciples, "Let us go into Judea again."

His disciples said to Him, "Master, lately the Jews have been trying to stone You, and will You go there again?"

But Jesus was not afraid to go. He knew that if He did what His Father in heaven wanted Him to do, His Father would take care of Him. Jesus would not die before the hour came that He should die. He said to the disciples, "Our friend Lazarus is sleeping, but I am going so that I may waken him out of sleep."

The disciples said, "Lord, if he sleeps, he shall do well."

When Jesus said he was sleeping, He was speaking of his death. Lazarus had died. The disciples thought that Jesus meant Lazarus was taking a rest by sleeping. Therefore Jesus plainly said to them, "Lazarus is dead. I am glad for your sakes that I was not there, in order that you might believe. Nevertheless, let us go to him."

Thomas said to the other disciples, "Let us also go so that we may die with Him."

When Jesus came to Bethany, He found that Lazarus had already been lying in the grave four days. Many of the Jews had come to visit the sisters and bring them words of comfort.

As soon as Martha heard that Jesus was coming, she went out to meet Him, but Mary stayed sitting in the house. When Martha came to Jesus, she said, "Lord, if You had been here, my brother would not have died. But I know that even now, whatever You will ask of God, God will give it to You."

Jesus said to Martha, "Your brother shall rise again."

Martha said, "I know that he shall rise again in the resurrection at the last day."

Jesus said to her, "I am the Resurrection and the Life. He who believes in Me, though he were dead, yet shall he live. And whoever lives and believes in Me shall never die. Do you believe this?"

Martha said to Him, "Yes, Lord, I believe that You

are the Christ, the Son of God who should come into the world." When Martha had said these words, she went back to the house and spoke secretly to her sister Mary. "The Master has come and is calling for you."

As soon as Mary heard this, she quickly got up and went to meet Jesus. He was still outside the city of Bethany where Martha had met Him.

When the Jews who were with Mary in the house saw her get up and leave so hastily, they followed her. They thought she was going to the grave to weep for Lazarus.

Mary had come to where Jesus was. When she saw Him, she fell down at His feet and said to Him, "Lord, if You had been here, my brother would not have died."

Jesus was troubled as He saw Mary weeping, and the Jews who had come with her also weeping. He said, "Where have you laid him?"

They said to Him, "Lord, come and see."

Jesus wept. Then the Jews said, "Behold how He loved him!"

Some of the people said, "Could not this Man, who opened the eyes of the blind, have caused that even this man should not have died?"

Jesus groaned within Himself. The people still did not understand His work or His ways. He came to the grave which was a cave with a stone laid at its mouth. Jesus said, "Take away the stone."

Martha said to Him, "Lord, by this time there will be a stench, for he has been dead four days.

Jesus said to her, "Did I not tell you that if you believe, you will see the glory of God?"

Then they took away the stone from the place where the body of Lazarus had been laid. Jesus lifted up His eyes and said, "Father, I thank You that You have heard Me. And I know that You always hear Me. But because of the people that stand by I said it, so that they may believe that You have sent me." Then Jesus cried with a loud voice, "Lazarus, come forth."

And Lazarus came out of the grave! He was wrapped tightly in grave clothes and had a napkin wrapped around his face. Jesus said, "Loosen him and let him go."

When the Jews who had come to Mary saw this great miracle, many of them believed on Jesus.

"Blessed Is the King of Israel!"

John 11:46–12:18

Many people believed in Jesus when they saw the miracle He had done in raising Lazarus from the dead. But there were still many who did not believe. Some of these went to the Pharisees and told them what Jesus had done.

The chief priests and the Pharisees gathered together to discuss these things. They said, "What shall we do? This Man is doing many miracles. If we let Him alone, all men will believe on Him. Then the Romans will come and take away both our place and nation."

Caiaphas, who was the high priest that year, said to them, "You do not know anything at all. You do not consider that it is necessary for us that one man should die for the people, and that the whole nation should not perish."

Caiaphas did not say this by his own wisdom. Because he was the high priest, God gave him the wisdom to foretell that Jesus should die for the Jewish people. He would die not for them only, but for the Gentile people also. Jesus would gather together all people who were the children of God, whether they were Jews or Gentiles.

From that day on, the Jewish leaders counseled together on how they might put Jesus to death.

Because of this, Jesus did not walk openly among the Jews. He went from there to a city called Ephraim in a country near the wilderness, and there He stayed with His disciples.

The time of the year that the Jews held their Passover was drawing near again, and many people went up to Jerusalem before the Passover to purify themselves. The Jews looked for Jesus to see whether they could find Him there. As they stood in the temple, they talked among themselves, saying, "What do you think? Will He come to the feast?"

Both the chief priests and the Pharisees had given a commandment that if anyone knew where Jesus was, he should let them know so that they could arrest Him.

Six days before the Passover, Jesus came back to Bethany where Lazarus was, whom He had raised from the dead. There they made a supper for Him. Martha did the serving, but Lazarus was one of those at the table with Jesus.

As Jesus sat at the table, Mary came with a pound of ointment of spikenard, a very expensive ointment. With this she anointed the feet of Jesus, and then she wiped His feet with her hair. The house was filled with the odor of the ointment.

Judas Iscariot, the disciple who was going to betray Jesus, was displeased. He said, "Why was this ointment not sold for three hundred pence and the money given to the poor?" Three hundred pence was about one year's wages at that time.

Judas did not say this because he cared for the poor people, but because he was a thief. He was the disciple in charge of the money bag. Perhaps he wanted more money to put into the bag so that he would have more to steal.

Jesus said, "Let her alone. She has done this ahead of time for my burial. You will always have the poor people with you, but you will not always have Me."

Many of the Jews heard that Jesus was at the house where a supper had been made for Him. They came there too, not only to see Jesus, but also to see Lazarus, whom Jesus had raised from the dead.

A large number of people believed on the Lord because of Lazarus. He was a reminder to them of Jesus' mighty power. But the chief priests counseled together on how they might also put Lazarus to death.

The next day Jesus went to Jerusalem. When many people who were there for the feast heard that He was coming, they took branches of palm trees and went out to meet Him. They cried, "Hosanna! Blessed is the King of Israel who comes in the Name of the Lord!"

Jesus found a young donkey and sat on it. This was to fulfill what the Old Testament Scriptures said about Him. The book of Zechariah says, "Rejoice greatly, O daughter of Zion; . . . behold, thy King cometh unto thee . . . riding . . . upon a colt, the foal of an ass."

At first the disciples did not understand this. But

when Jesus was glorified, they remembered that this was written in the Scriptures about Him and that they had done these things to Him.

Some of the people had been with Jesus when He raised Lazarus from the dead, and they had told many others about that miracle. This was another reason that such a great crowd came to meet Jesus when He rode into Jerusalem.

Death Leads to Life

John 12:19–43

It angered the Pharisees to see the people coming to Jesus. They had said that if anyone knew where Jesus was, he should tell them so that they could arrest Him. Now instead, many people were crowding around Jesus. The Pharisees said among themselves, "Do you see how we are not succeeding in anything? Look, the world has gone after Him."

Certain men who were not Jews had come to the feast to worship. They came to Philip, who was from Bethsaida in Galilee, and brought him this request: "Sir, we would like to see Jesus."

Philip went to Andrew and told him what they had asked, and then both Andrew and Philip went and told Jesus.

Jesus said to them, "The hour has come that the Son of Man should be glorified." Then He gave them an illustration of how it is when a kernel of wheat is planted. If the kernel does not die, it cannot sprout and make a new plant to raise more wheat. It just stays in the ground. But if the little kernel dies, it sprouts and becomes a new plant and makes more wheat.

This is true with people, too. If a man will not give

up his self-will, his life is not worth much. But if he will die to his self-will, God will give him spiritual life.

Jesus knew what it is like to die to self. To face death for all the people was a hard thing for Him. His soul was troubled, and His flesh would have liked to be saved from that hour. But Jesus would not give in to this desire. He knew that the very purpose for which He had come into the world was to die. So He said instead, "Father, glorify Your Name."

When Jesus had said this, a voice came from heaven. "I have both glorified it and will glorify it again."

The people who stood near heard this voice, but they did not know what it was. Some people thought that it thundered. Others said that an angel had spoken to Him.

Jesus said to them, "This voice did not come because of Me, but for your sakes. Now is the judgment of this world. Now shall the prince of this world be cast out. And I, if I be lifted up from the earth, will draw all men to Myself."

Jesus was speaking about the kind of death He would die. He would be lifted up on a cross and there die for the sins of the people. Through His death, Satan would lose his power over those who put their trust in Jesus.

The people could not understand why Jesus should die if He is the Christ. They said, "We have heard from the Law that Christ lives forever. Then how do You say, 'The Son of Man must be lifted up'? Who is this Son of

Man?"

Jesus told them, "Yet a little while is the Light with you. Walk in the light while you have it, lest darkness should come upon you. For he who walks in darkness does not know where he is going." With these words He urged them to follow Him, who is Light, so that they would know where they were going. Then Jesus went away and hid Himself from them.

Even though Jesus had done so many miracles among them, still they did not believe in Him. In the Book of Isaiah, the prophet foretold that it would be this way. They did not really want to know, so they could not know. Oh, yes, they pretended that they wanted to know, and if Jesus' way would have fitted into their plans, they would have wanted to know. But they loved themselves too much to give up their own ways.

Even among the chief rulers of the Jews there were some who believed that Jesus is the Son of God. But they would not confess that they believed, for they were afraid that the Pharisees would put them out of the synagogue. These secret believers loved the favor of the Pharisees more than the favor of God.

The Last Supper

John 13:1–35

As the Feast of the Passover drew near, Jesus knew that the time had come for Him to leave the world and go to His Father. He loved His disciples very much, for they were His own in the world. They had been willing to follow Him, and He loved them to the end.

Because Judas was not faithful to the Lord, Satan had the rule over him. He now put it into Judas's heart to betray Jesus; that is, to deliver Jesus to His enemies.

When the time came, Jesus ate the Passover supper with His twelve disciples. He also wanted to give the disciples a good example to follow after He was gone. So when the supper was over, Jesus got up and put off some of His outer clothes. He took a towel and fastened it around Himself. Then He poured water into a basin and began to wash the disciples' feet. He wiped them with the towel that He had tied around Himself.

When Jesus came to Simon Peter, Peter asked Him, "Lord, do You wash my feet?"

Jesus said, "You do not know now what I am doing, but you will know afterwards."

Peter said to Jesus, "You shall never wash my feet."

Jesus answered, "If I do not wash you, you have no

part with Me."

Peter wanted very much to belong to Jesus. If it would help to have his feet washed, he wanted to belong as much as he could. So he said, "Lord, wash not only my feet, but also my hands and my head."

But Jesus knew this was not necessary. "He who is already clean does not need to be washed, except for his feet," Jesus said. He was speaking about being clean from sin. People who have been cleansed from sin want to do everything that Jesus would have them do.

Then Jesus said, "You are clean, but not all." He said that because of Judas, whose heart was defiled with sin.

After Jesus had washed the disciples' feet, He put on His robes and sat down again. He asked them, "Do you know what I have done to you? You call Me Master and Lord, and it is well that you call Me that, for so I am. If I then, your Lord and Master, have washed your feet, you also ought to wash one another's feet. I have given you an example so that you should do as I have done to you. If you know these things, you will be happy if you do them."

Then Jesus became deeply troubled in His spirit. He told the disciples, "Verily, verily, I say to you that one of you shall betray Me."

Even though Jesus had always known that Judas would betray Him, the disciples did not know it. So when Jesus said this, they looked at one another to see if they could find out who it was.

The one who was near Jesus and leaning on His bosom said, "Lord, who is it?"

Jesus answered, "It is the one to whom I shall give a sop, when I have dipped it."

When Jesus had dipped the sop, He gave it to Judas Iscariot, the son of Simon.

After the sop, Satan entered into Judas. Then Jesus said to him, "What you do, do quickly."

No one at the table knew why Jesus said this to Judas. Some of them thought it was because Judas carried the money bag. Perhaps Jesus wanted him to buy the things that were needed for the feast. Or they thought it might be that He wanted Judas to give something to the poor.

As soon as Judas had received the sop, he immediately went out into the night.

Jesus had many things to say to His disciples before He left them. One thing He told them was that all men would know they were His disciples if they loved one another. He gave them the commandment to love one another as He had loved them. Jesus' love never fails, and His followers should never let their love for one another fail either.

Jesus Teaches the Troubled Disciples

John 13:33–15:11

Jesus said to the disciples, "Little children, yet a little while I am with you. You shall look for Me; and as I said to the Jews, 'Where I go, you cannot come,' I say the same to you."

Simon Peter said to Him, "Lord, where are You going?"

Jesus answered him, "Where I go, you cannot follow Me now, but you shall follow Me afterward."

Peter said, "Lord, why can I not follow You now? I am willing to die for Your sake."

Jesus answered him, "Will you die for My sake? Verily, verily, I say to you that the cock shall not crow till you have denied three times that you know Me."

Jesus knew that Peter's heart and the hearts of the other disciples were troubled because of the things He was telling them. He said, "Do not let your hearts be troubled. You believe in God; believe also in Me. In My Father's house are many mansions. If this were not true, I would have told you. I go to prepare a place for you. And if I go to prepare a place for you, I will come again and receive you to Myself so that where I am, there you may be also. You know where I am going, and you know the way."

Thomas said to Jesus, "Lord, we do not know where You are going, and how can we know the way?"

Jesus said, "I am the Way, the Truth and the Life. No man comes to the Father but by Me. If you had known Me, you should have known My Father also. From this time on you know Him and have seen Him."

Philip said to Him, "Lord, show us the Father, and that will satisfy us."

Jesus said to him, "Have I been with you so long, and yet you have not known Me, Philip? He who has seen Me has seen the Father. How then do you say, 'Show us the Father'? Do you not believe that I am in the Father and the Father in Me? The words that I speak to you, I do not speak of Myself, but the Father who dwells in Me, He does the works. Believe Me that I am in the Father and the Father in Me, or else believe Me for the very works' sake."

Jesus told the disciples that the people who believe on Him will also do the works that He does, and even greater works. If they will ask anything through His Name, God will do it for them, so that the Father may be glorified in the Son.

Jesus promised them that when He went away, He would not leave them without comfort. He would send them the Holy Spirit, the Comforter, to abide with them forever. The Holy Spirit would teach them all things and bring back to their memories the things that Jesus had taught them.

Jesus told His disciples these things so that when they came to pass, the disciples would believe. Later when the Holy Ghost brought to their memory the things Jesus had taught, those things were written down. We can read them today in the Bible.

Jesus told the disciples a story to help them understand a truth He wanted to teach them. He used the example of a vine to illustrate the truth. The branches on a vine stay alive as long as they receive life from the vine. But if they do not receive life from the vine, the branches die and no longer bear fruit. Men gather the dead branches and burn them, because they are useless apart from the vine. Even the branches that are on the vine and bearing fruit need to be pruned or trimmed so that they will bear more fruit.

Jesus said, "I am the true Vine, and My Father is the caretaker. You are the branches. If you continue to receive life from Me, you will bring forth fruit. The Father will prune you so that you will bring forth more and better fruit. If a man does not abide in Me, he will be cut off and cast away as a dead branch.

"My Father is glorified when you bring forth much fruit. Keep My commandments, and you will abide in My love. I have told you these things so that your joy might be full."

Jesus Prepares the Disciples

John 15:14–17:26

Jesus said to His disciples, "You are My friends if you do whatever I tell you to do. From now on I will not call you servants. Servants do not know everything their masters are doing. But I have made known to you all the things that My Father has told Me. You have not chosen Me, but I have chosen you and ordained you so that you should go and bring forth fruit that will last.

"Do not be surprised if the world hates you," said Jesus. "If the world hates Me, it will also hate My disciples. If you were like the world, the world would love you. But because I have chosen you to be separate from the world, the world hates you."

Then Jesus told the disciples that they would be put out of the synagogues for His sake. Yes, the time would even come when the people who killed them would think they were doing the will of God.

When the disciples heard these things and understood that Jesus was going away, their hearts were filled with sorrow. But Jesus told them the truth anyway. That was the best way to prepare them to face the hard things that would come. Jesus also promised to send them another Comforter, the Holy Ghost. He would help them and comfort them in their troubles.

Jesus had many more things to tell the disciples, but their hearts were already so full of sorrow that they were not able to bear more at this time. So He said, "When the Spirit of Truth has come, He will guide you into all truth. He will teach you all the things you still need to know."

Jesus said, "A little while, and you shall not see Me, and again a little while, and you shall see Me, because I go to the Father."

The disciples talked about this among themselves. "What is this that He says to us, 'A little while, and you shall not see Me, and again a little while, and you shall see Me'; and 'Because I go to the Father'? We cannot understand what He means."

Jesus knew that they wanted to ask Him about this, so He explained it further. "Verily, verily, I tell you that you will weep and mourn, but the world will rejoice. You will be sorrowful, but your sorrow will be turned to joy."

When Jesus died, the world would rejoice to be rid of Him, but the disciples would be in great sorrow. When Jesus rose again, the disciples would rejoice, for Jesus would then be alive forevermore.

The disciples were glad when Jesus spoke more plainly to them. They said, "Now we are sure that You know all things. You are able to answer questions before anyone even asks You. By this we know that You came from God."

Jesus answered, "Do you believe now? Behold, the

hour is coming, yes, is now come, that you shall be scattered and shall leave Me alone. Yet I am not alone, for the Father is with Me. I have told you these things so that you might have peace in Me. In the world you will have trouble, but be of good cheer, I have overcome the world."

When Jesus said these words, He lifted up His eyes and prayed to His Father in heaven. First He prayed for Himself. Next He prayed for His disciples, and then He prayed for others who would believe on Him through the disciples' words.

Jesus Betrayed and Arrested

John 18:1–27

When Jesus had finished praying, He went with His disciples over the Brook Kidron, where there was a garden. Jesus entered this garden with the disciples. Because He and the disciples often went there, Judas also knew about this place and knew where to find Jesus.

In the meantime, Judas had gone to the chief priests and officers and made an agreement with them. He would betray Jesus to them if they would give him money for it. The chief priests and Pharisees gave Judas a band of men and officers to go with him and arrest Jesus. They came with their lanterns and torches and weapons to where Jesus was.

Because Jesus already knew about everything that would happen, He went out to meet the officers. He said, "Whom do you seek?"

They answered, "Jesus of Nazareth."

Jesus answered, "I am He."

As soon as Jesus said, "I am He," the men went backward and fell to the ground. This showed the power of Jesus' words. The men could not take Him by force against His will. Most prisoners would have tried to run away, but Jesus gave Himself to them.

Jesus asked them again, "Whom do you seek?"

They said, "Jesus of Nazareth."

Jesus answered, "I have told you that I am He. So if you are looking for Me, let these go their way."

Simon Peter had a sword along with him, and he decided to use it. Down it came against the head of the high priest's servant, and it cut off his right ear. The servant's name was Malchus. Poor Malchus suddenly lost an ear—but not for long. Jesus touched the place where the ear had been and healed him.

Jesus said to Peter, "Put up your sword into the sheath. The cup which My Father has given Me, shall I not drink it?"

Peter wanted to defend Jesus and fight His enemies for Him. But Jesus was willing to bear the suffering that was His Father's will for Him. His kindness was an example for His followers, whom He had taught to love their enemies.

The band of men and the captain and the officers of the Jews took Jesus and bound Him. First they led Him away to Annas. He was the father-in-law of Caiaphas, who was the high priest that year.

Simon Peter and another disciple followed Jesus. The other disciple was known by the high priest, and he went along into the house. But Peter stood outside the door. The other disciple, whom the high priest knew, went out and spoke to the girl who was the doorkeeper. She let the other disciple take Peter along inside with him.

The girl who kept the door said to Peter, "Are you not also one of this Man's disciples?"

Peter denied it, saying, "I am not."

Because it was cold, the servants and officers had made a fire of coals. As they stood there and warmed themselves, Peter stood with them and also warmed himself.

Then the high priest asked Jesus about His disciples and about His teaching.

Jesus answered him, "I spoke openly to the world. I always taught in the synagogue and in the temple where the Jews regularly come together. In secret have I done nothing. Why do you ask Me? Ask those who heard what I have said to them. Behold, they know what I said."

When Jesus had said this, one of the officers who stood by struck Jesus with the palm of his hand. "Do You answer the high priest like that?" he asked.

Jesus answered him, "If I have spoken evil, tell about the evil. But if I have spoken right, why do you strike Me?"

Then Annas sent Jesus bound to Caiaphas.

Simon Peter was standing and warming himself at the fire. Some of those who were there asked him, "Are you also one of His disciples?"

"I am not," Peter declared.

One of the servants standing there was a relative of the man whose ear Peter had cut off. He said, "Did I not see you in the garden with Him?"

Peter then denied it again, and immediately the cock crowed.

Jesus Before Pilate

John 18:28–19:12

That night Jesus was tried before Caiaphas and sentenced to death. But the Jews would get into trouble with the Roman government if they put a man to death themselves. They needed to get permission from the governor. Therefore, early in the morning they led Jesus from Caiaphas to the Hall of Judgment.

But the Jews themselves would not go into the Hall of Judgment. It was near the time to eat the Feast of the Passover, and they wanted to be clean for that. They would not defile themselves by going into the Judgment Hall of the Romans. How sad that they should be so particular about being clean for the Passover, but not realize how unclean their hearts were in hating the Son of God.

Pilate, the governor, had to go out to the Jews to talk to them because they would not come in. He asked them, "What accusation do you bring against this Man?"

They answered, "If He were not an evildoer, we would not have delivered Him to you."

Then Pilate said to them, "You take Him and judge Him according to your law."

The Jews said to Pilate, "It is not lawful for us to put any man to death."

Pilate went back into the Judgment Hall. He called Jesus and asked Him, "Are You the King of the Jews?"

Jesus answered, "Are you saying this of yourself, or did others tell you this about Me?"

"Am I a Jew?" asked Pilate. "Your own nation and the chief priests have delivered You to me. What have You done?"

Jesus answered, "My kingdom is not of this world. If My kingdom were of this world, then My servants would fight so that I should not be delivered to the Jews. But now My kingdom is not from here."

"So You are a king, then?" Pilate asked.

Jesus answered, "You say that I am a king. For this purpose I was born, and for this cause I came into the world, that I should show the truth. Everyone who is of the truth listens to My voice."

"What is truth?" asked Pilate. Then he went out again to the Jews and said, "I find no fault in Him. But you have a custom that I set one of your prisoners free at the Passover. So do you want me to release the King of the Jews for you?"

Of course they did not! They cried out, "Not this Man, but Barabbas!" Now Barabbas was a robber and a murderer.

Then Pilate had his soldiers whip Jesus terribly. They braided a crown of thorns and put it on His head, and they put a purple robe on Him. They made fun of

Him, saying, "Hail, King of the Jews!" They also hit Him with their hands.

Jesus went out, wearing the crown of thorns and the purple robe. Pilate said to the Jews, "Behold the Man!"

When the chief priests and officers saw Him, they cried out, "Crucify Him, crucify Him!"

Pilate said to them, "You take Him and crucify Him, because I do not find any fault in Him."

The Jews answered Pilate, "We have a law, and by our law He ought to die because He made Himself the Son of God."

When Pilate heard this, he was all the more afraid. He went into the Judgment Hall again and said to Jesus, "Where are You from?"

Jesus gave him no answer.

Then Pilate said to Jesus, "Do You not speak to me? Do You not know that I have power to crucify You and power to free You?"

Jesus said, "You could have no power against Me unless it were given to you from above. Because of this, he who delivered Me to you has the greater sin."

Then Pilate tried even harder to find a way to release Jesus. But the Jews cried out, "If you let this Man go, you are not Caesar's friend. Whoever makes himself a king is speaking against Caesar."

Caesar was the Roman king who ruled over the Jews at this time. The Jews did not appreciate being under his rule and would have liked to be free. If Jesus had been against Caesar and had freed them from his rule, the Jews would have been glad. But they were not willing to let Him free them from their sins. Now, in order to have Jesus killed, they were pretending to be friends of Caesar.

Jesus Gives His Life

John 19:13–42

Pilate might be in trouble for showing that he was not Caesar's friend, yet he did not want to be guilty of condemning an innocent man to death. Pilate brought Jesus out to the people and said, "Behold your King!"

But they cried out, "Away with Him, away with Him! Crucify Him!"

Pilate said to them, "Shall I crucify your King?"

The chief priests answered, "We have no king but Caesar."

Then Pilate delivered Jesus to the Jews to have Him crucified. They took Jesus and led Him away.

Jesus, carrying His cross, went out to a place called the place of a skull. There they crucified Him with two other men, one on each side of Him and Jesus in the middle.

Pilate wrote a title to be put on the cross. This was the title he wrote: "JESUS OF NAZARETH, THE KING OF THE JEWS."

Many of the Jews read this title because the place where Jesus was crucified was near the city. The title was written in three different languages: Hebrew, Greek, and Latin.

The Jewish chief priests said to Pilate, "Do not write 'The King of the Jews,' but that He said, 'I am the King of the Jews.'"

But Pilate would not change it for them. He said, "What I have written, I have written."

The soldiers who crucified Jesus took His clothes and divided them into four parts, and each soldier received one part. But His coat could not very well be divided because it had been woven as one piece without any seams. So they said among themselves, "Let us not tear it, but cast lots for it, to see whose it shall be."

When the soldiers did this, they were fulfilling the words of an Old Testament Scripture that says, "They parted my raiment among them, and for my vesture they did cast lots."

The enemies of Jesus were not the only ones at the scene of His crucifixion. Several women who loved Jesus were there too. Among them were His mother, His mother's sister, Mary the wife of Cleophas, and Mary Magdalene.

When Jesus saw His mother and the disciple whom He loved standing by, He said to His mother, "Woman, behold your son!" And to the disciple He said, "Behold your mother!" From that time on that disciple took Mary into his own home.

Then in order to fulfill the Scriptures, Jesus said, "I thirst."

A vessel full of vinegar was there. They filled a sponge with the vinegar, put it upon a branch of hyssop, and gave it to Jesus to drink.

When Jesus had received the vinegar, He said, "It is finished." Then He bowed His head and gave up His life.

Because it was so near the time of the Passover, the Jews did not want the bodies hanging on the crosses on the Sabbath Day. The Sabbath Day at the time of the Passover was a special day for them. So they asked Pilate to have the legs of Jesus and the two thieves broken. If their legs were broken, they would die sooner. Then the bodies could be taken down and buried before the end of the day.

The soldiers came and broke the legs of the first thief who was crucified with Jesus, and then the legs of the other thief. When they came to Jesus, they saw that He was dead already, so they did not break His legs. But one of the soldiers pierced His side with a spear, and out of Jesus' side came blood and water.

The one who saw this made a record of it. His record is true, and it is written so that we might believe. These things also happened according to the Scriptures. In Psalms it says, "A bone of him shall not be broken." In another Scripture it says, "They shall look on him whom they pierced."

After this, Joseph of Arimathaea went to Pilate. Joseph was a disciple of Jesus, but he had kept it secret because he was afraid of the Jews. Now he begged Pilate that he might take away the body of Jesus, and Pilate gave him permission. So Joseph came and took Jesus' body down from the cross.

Nicodemus, who had talked with Jesus at night, also came with a mixture of spices and perfumes. They took the body of Jesus and wrapped it in linen cloths with the spices. It was the custom of the Jews to do this when they buried people.

In the place where Jesus was crucified there was a garden. In the garden was a new sepulcher in which no one had ever before been buried. Here they laid Jesus' body, for the time of the Passover was near and the place was close at hand.

Joy After Sorrow

John 20

It was Sunday morning, the day after the Sabbath Day and the first day of the week. That morning while it was still dark, Mary Magdalene came to the place where Jesus had been buried. To her great surprise, she saw that the stone was taken away from the sepulcher!

Mary ran and found Simon Peter and the other disciple whom Jesus loved. She said to them, "They have taken the Lord out of the sepulcher, and we do not know where they have laid Him."

So Peter and the other disciple started off together, running to the sepulcher. The other disciple outran Peter and came first to the sepulcher. Stooping down, he saw the linen clothes lying inside, but he did not go in.

Simon Peter came following, and he went into the sepulcher. He saw the linen clothes and the napkin that had been wrapped around Jesus' head. The napkin was not lying with the linen clothes, but was wrapped together in a place by itself.

Then John, the other disciple who had come first, also went into the sepulcher. When he saw the graveclothes, he believed what Mary had said. They still did not know the Scriptures that said Jesus must rise again from the dead. Then the disciples went away to their own homes.

But Mary stood outside the sepulcher, weeping. As she wept, she stooped down and looked into the sepulcher. There she saw two angels sitting, the one at the head and the other at the feet, where the body of Jesus had lain.

The angels asked her, "Woman, why do you weep?"

She said, "Because they have taken away my Lord, and I do not know where they have laid Him."

When she had said this, she turned around and saw Jesus standing there. But she did not know that it was Jesus.

Jesus said to her, "Woman, why are you weeping? Whom are you seeking?"

Mary supposed that this was the man who took care of the garden. So she said to Him, "Sir, if you have carried Him away from here, tell me where you have laid Him, and I will take Him away."

Jesus said to her, "Mary."

She turned and said to Him, "Master!"

Jesus said to her, "Do not touch Me, for I am not yet ascended to My Father. But go to My brethren and say to them, 'I ascend to My Father and your Father, and to My God and your God.'"

Mary Magdalene went and told the disciples that she had seen the Lord, and she told them what He had said to her.

That same day, in the evening of the first day of the

week, the disciples gathered together behind closed doors because they were afraid of the Jews. Suddenly Jesus appeared, standing in the midst of them, and He said, "Peace be to you." Then He showed them His hands and His side.

The disciples were glad when they saw the Lord.

Jesus said to them again, "Peace be to you. As My Father has sent Me, even so send I you." When He had said this, He breathed on them and said, "Receive the Holy Ghost. Whoever's sins you forgive will be forgiven them, and whoever's sins you do not forgive will be held against them."

Thomas was not in the group when Jesus appeared to them. The other ten disciples told him that they had seen the Lord. But Thomas said, "Unless I shall see in His hands the print of the nails and thrust my hand into His side, I will not believe."

Eight days later the disciples were again together behind closed doors. This time Thomas was with them. Jesus came and stood in the midst of them and said, "Peace be to you." Then He said to Thomas, "Reach here your finger, and see My hand; and reach here your hand, and thrust it into My side. And do not be faithless, but believing."

Thomas saw and believed that it was Jesus. He said, "My Lord and my God."

Jesus said, "Thomas, because you have seen Me, you have believed. Blessed are they who have not seen and yet have believed."

Jesus did many other signs in the presence of His disciples that John did not write in the Book of John. But the things he did write were recorded so that we might believe that Jesus is the Christ, the Son of God.

Jesus and the Disciples at the Seashore
John 21

There was another time when Jesus showed Himself to the disciples after His resurrection. Simon Peter, Thomas, Nathanael, James and John, and two other disciples were at the Sea of Galilee. Simon Peter said to the others, "I am going fishing."

They said to him, "We will go with you." So immediately they went and got into a ship, but that night they caught nothing.

In the morning Jesus stood on the shore, but the disciples did not know that it was Jesus. Jesus said to them, "Children, have you any meat?"

They answered Him, "No."

Jesus said to them, "Throw the net on the other side of the ship, and you will find." They threw out the net on the right side, and now they caught so many fish that they were not able to draw the net into the boat.

The disciple whom Jesus loved said to Peter, "It is the Lord." When Simon Peter heard that, he put on his fisher's coat, threw himself into the sea, and swam to shore.

The other disciples were not far from land. They brought the little ship to land, dragging the net with the fish.

As soon as they had come to land, they saw a fire of coals there. Some fish were laid on the coals, and some bread was there also. Jesus said to them, "Bring some of the fish that you have caught."

Simon Peter went up and drew the net to land, full of great fish. Altogether there were one hundred fifty-three of them, and yet with all these fish the net was not broken.

Jesus said to them, "Come and dine."

None of the disciples dared ask Him, "Who are You?" knowing that it was the Lord.

Then Jesus served them bread and fish.

This was the third time that Jesus showed Himself to His disciples after He had risen from the dead.

When they had eaten, Jesus said to Simon Peter, "Simon, son of Jonas, do you love Me more than these?"

Peter answered, "Yes, Lord, you know that I love You."

"Feed My lambs," said Jesus.

A second time Jesus said to Peter, "Simon, son of Jonas, do you love Me?"

Peter said, "Yes, Lord, You know that I love You."

"Feed My sheep," said Jesus.

A third time Jesus asked, "Simon, son of Jonas, do you love Me?"

Peter was grieved because Jesus asked him the third time, "Do you love Me?" He said to Jesus, "Lord, You know all things. You know that I love You."

Jesus said to him, "Feed My sheep. Verily, verily, I say to you that when you were young, you dressed yourself and walked where you wanted to walk. But when you are old, you will stretch out your hands and another shall dress you and carry you where you do not want to go."

In saying this, Jesus was speaking about the kind of death Peter would die and thereby glorify God. Then Jesus said to Peter, "Follow Me."

Peter turned around and saw the disciple whom Jesus loved following. He was the one who had been close to Jesus at the Passover meal and had asked, "Lord, who is he who betrays You?"

Seeing him, Peter said to Jesus, "Lord, and what shall this man do?"

Jesus said to him, "If I will that he tarries till I come, what is that to you? You follow Me."

Then it was said among the brethren that this disciple would not die. But that is not exactly what Jesus had said. He had only said, "If I will that he tarries till I come, what is that to you?"

This disciple was John, the writer of the fourth book of the Gospel. He told and wrote about these things, and we know that the things he wrote are true.

There were also many other things that Jesus did. John supposed that if everything were written about Jesus that could be written, even the world itself could not hold all the books that should be written.

Unit Two

The Book of Acts

Introduction to Acts

During the time of the Book of Acts, Roman emperors ruled Palestine and all the nearby countries. (Palestine is the land that was earlier called Canaan and was given to the Jews.) Most of these Roman rulers were called Caesars. They lived in the city of Rome in the country of Italy.

Augustus Caesar was the emperor when Jesus was born. Then a few years after Jesus' visit to Jerusalem at the age of twelve, Tiberius Caesar became the emperor. He ruled until some time after Jesus' death. Claudius Caesar became the next emperor, and he was the Roman ruler during most of the happenings of the Book of Acts. Nero is not mentioned in the Book of Acts, but he was ruler during the last part of Paul's life.

The land of Palestine was divided into different sections, and different rulers were put over these sections by the Romans. Several of these rulers were of a family named Herod. We read of two Herods in the Book of Acts. The first one is Herod Agrippa, and the other one is Herod Agrippa the Second.

Besides these, there were other rulers that the Romans put over Palestine from time to time. But the Jews were tired of being under Roman rule. They looked forward to the time when their own kingdom could again be restored to them.

The man who wrote the Gospel according to Luke also wrote the Book of Acts. This book comes after the four Gospels, which tell about Jesus' work here on earth. The Book of Acts was written to tell about the continuing work of Jesus through the apostles after Jesus had gone back to heaven.

The Ascension of Jesus

Acts 1

After Jesus rose from the dead, He showed the apostles that He was alive by many proofs that could not be denied. For forty days they saw Jesus from time to time, and He spoke to them about the kingdom of God.

Then Jesus met with the apostles on the Mount of Olives, which is a Sabbath Day's journey from Jerusalem. He told them to wait at Jerusalem for the promise of the Father which He had told them about. "For John indeed baptized with water," Jesus said. "But you will be baptized with the Holy Spirit not many days from now."

The apostles asked Him, "Lord, will You at this time restore again the kingdom to Israel?"

Jesus said, "It is not for you to know when these things will happen. The Father has these things in His own power. But you shall receive power after the Holy

Ghost has come upon you. Then you shall be witnesses to Me both in Jerusalem, and in Judea, and in Samaria, and to the uttermost part of the earth."

When Jesus had spoken these things, while they were watching, He was taken up, and a cloud received Him out of their sight. While they kept looking toward heaven as He went up, two men in white clothing stood by them. They said, "You men of Galilee, why do you stand gazing up into heaven? This same Jesus, who has been taken up from you into heaven, shall so come in the same way that you have seen Him go into heaven."

Then the apostles returned to Jerusalem, where they stayed in an upper room. Their names were Peter, James, John, Andrew, Philip, Thomas, Bartholomew, Matthew, James the son of Alphaeus, Simon Zelotes, and Judas the brother of James. These all continued together in prayer and supplication along with the women, and Mary the mother of Jesus, and Jesus' brothers.

During these days Peter stood up in the midst of the disciples. All together about one hundred twenty of them were present. Peter said, "Men and brethren, this Scripture needs to be fulfilled which the Holy Ghost by the mouth of David spoke about Judas, who betrayed Jesus. For he was numbered with us and had obtained part of this ministry.

"Now this man bought a field with the reward of sin; and falling down headfirst, he burst open and all his bowels gushed out. This became so widely known among the dwellers at Jerusalem that the field is called the 'field of blood.' For it is written in the Book of Psalms, 'Let his place be emptied, let no man dwell in it, and let another man take his office.' Therefore, of these men who have been with us all the time from the baptism of John until Jesus was taken up from us, someone must be ordained to be a witness with us of His resurrection."

Then they appointed two men. One was Joseph, who also had the names Barsabas and Justus. The other was Matthias. The disciples realized that the Lord knew better than they which one should take the place of Judas. So they prayed, "You, Lord, who know the hearts of all men, show which of these two men You have chosen. Then he may take part of this ministry and apostleship from which Judas fell, that he might go to his own place."

And they cast lots, and the lot fell upon Matthias. From then on he was numbered with the other eleven as an apostle of Jesus.

The Day of Pentecost

Acts 2

Ten days after Jesus had ascended into heaven was the day of Pentecost. This was a feast that the Jews held fifty days after the Feast of the Passover. On this day all the disciples in Jerusalem were together in one place.

Suddenly there came a sound from heaven like a rushing mighty wind, and it filled the whole house where they were sitting. Then there appeared to them divided tongues as though they were of fire, and the tongues sat upon each of them. All the disciples were filled with the Holy Ghost, and they began to speak in other languages as the Spirit gave them words to speak.

Many sincere, religious Jews from many different nations were in Jerusalem. When the news spread of what had just happened, the multitude gathered around the disciples. They were greatly perplexed and confused because each man heard the message in his own language. In wonder and amazement they said, "Look, are not all these who speak Galileans? How can we all understand them in our own language in which we were born? For we hear them speaking in our languages the wonderful works of God."

The people stood there astonished and confounded

about what was going on. They said one to another, "What does this mean?"

Others mocked the disciples. "These men are full of new wine," they said.

But Peter, standing up with the other apostles, raised his voice and said, "You men of Judea, and all you who dwell at Jerusalem, listen to my words. These men are not drunk as you suppose, for it is only nine o'clock in the morning. But this is what the prophet Joel spoke about, 'And it shall come to pass in the last days, says God, that I will pour out My Spirit upon all flesh. Your sons and your daughters shall prophesy, your young men shall see visions, and your old men shall dream dreams. And on My servants and handmaidens I will pour out in those days of My Spirit, and they shall prophesy. And I will show wonders in heaven above and signs in the earth beneath—blood, and fire, and vapor of smoke. The sun shall be turned into darkness and the moon into blood, before that great and notable day of the Lord comes. And it shall come to pass that whoever will call on the Name of the Lord shall be saved.'

"You men of Israel, listen to these words. Jesus of Nazareth lived as a Man among you. He was approved of God by miracles and wonders and signs, which God did by Him in your presence, as you know. According to the plan and foreknowledge of God, you took Him; and by wicked hands you crucified and killed Him. But God has raised Him up, because it was not possible that death should keep Him. David also spoke about

His resurrection in the Book of Psalms when he said that His soul was not left in the place of the dead, neither did His flesh decay.

"This Jesus has God raised up, and we are all witnesses of it. He has sent forth the Holy Spirit, which is the reason for what you see and hear today. Therefore, let all the house of Israel know for certain that God has made this same Jesus, whom you have crucified, both Lord and Christ."

When the people heard these words, they were pricked in their heart. They felt so guilty that they asked, "Men and brethren, what shall we do?"

Peter said, "Repent and be baptized, every one of you, in the Name of Jesus Christ for the forgiveness of sins, and you shall receive the gift of the Holy Ghost. For the promise is to you and to your children, and to all who are far away, as many as the Lord our God shall call."

Peter said many other things also, testifying for God and warning the people. Then those who gladly received the Word were baptized, and that same day about three thousand believers were added to the group. The believers listened willingly to the teaching of the apostles and continued in fellowship and prayer with them. The apostles also did many signs and wonders among the people.

All those who believed stayed together, and they shared whatever they owned. Many sold their possessions and divided the money among the believers.

In this way they took care of everyone's needs. Day by day they came to the temple and worshiped together. They ate at the different houses and praised God with gladness of heart, and they were in favor with all the people.

The Lord added to the church daily those who were being saved.

Peter and John in the Temple

Acts 3:1–4:31

One day Peter and John were going to the temple at three o'clock, which was the hour of prayer. There they saw a certain man who had been lame ever since he was born. Every day he was laid at the temple gate which was called Beautiful, and there he would ask for money from the people who went into the temple. The people gave him alms, or money for the poor.

When the lame man saw Peter and John about to go into the temple, he asked them for alms. Peter fixed his eyes on the lame man and said, "Look at us."

The lame man had good hopes of receiving money from Peter and John, so he gave heed to them. But Peter said, "I do not have any silver or gold, but what I do have I will give to you. In the Name of Jesus Christ of Nazareth, rise up and walk."

Peter took the lame man by his right hand and lifted him up. Immediately his feet and ankle bones received strength, and he leaped to his feet. The man went into the temple with Peter and John, walking and leaping and praising God. He had truly received something much better than money. He had received healing!

All the people saw him walking and praising God,

and they knew that he was the man who had sat begging for alms at the Beautiful gate of the temple. As the healed man held on to Peter and John, all the people ran together to them in the porch that was called Solomon's. They were filled with wonder and amazement at this great miracle that had been performed.

When Peter saw what a gathering and stir this was causing, he said, "You men of Israel, why do you marvel at this? Why do you look so earnestly at us, as though by our own power or holiness we had made this man to walk? The God of Abraham, Isaac and Jacob, the God of our fathers, has glorified His Son Jesus. He is the same Jesus whom you delivered up, and denied in the presence of Pilate, when he was determined to let Him go. But you denied the Holy One and the Just, and desired a murderer to be granted to you. You killed the Prince of Life, whom God has raised from the dead. It is through His Name and through believing in His Name that this man is made strong. Yes, faith in His Name has given him this perfect soundness in the presence of you all.

"And now, brethren, I know that through ignorance you did it, as also did your rulers. But those things that God made known before by the words of the prophets, that Christ should suffer, He has brought to pass. Repent therefore, and be converted so that your sins may be blotted out."

As Peter and John continued preaching to the people, the priests, the captain of the temple, and the

Sadducees came upon them. These men were greatly disturbed that the apostles were teaching the people and preaching through Jesus the resurrection from the dead. The Sadducees did not believe in a resurrection. They thought that after people die, they remain dead and never rise again.

Peter and John were arrested and put into prison until the next day, because it was already evening. Yet many of the people who heard the Word believed, and now the number of disciples came to about five thousand men.

The next day the rulers, elders, and scribes gathered together with Annas the high priest, Caiaphas, John, Alexander, and the relatives of the high priest. Then they brought Peter and John into the midst of the council. "By what power or by what name have you healed this lame man?" they asked.

Peter, filled with the Holy Ghost, said to them, "You rulers of the people and elders of Israel: If we are being examined today because of the good deed done to the lame man and how he is made well, let it be known that by the Name of Jesus Christ of Nazareth, whom you crucified and God raised from the dead, even by Him does this man stand well before you. This is the Stone which was rejected by you builders and which has become the head of the corner. Neither is there salvation in any other, for there is no other name under heaven given among men whereby we must be saved."

The rulers knew that Peter and John were unlearned

and ignorant men. When they saw the boldness of these men, they marveled. They realized that such boldness could only come from having been with Jesus.

Seeing the man who was healed standing with them, they could say nothing against it. Facts were facts. The proof was there. They commanded Peter and John to leave the council, and then they discussed things among themselves.

"What shall we do to these men?" they asked. "For indeed they have done a remarkable miracle. Everyone who lives in Jerusalem knows it, and we cannot deny it. But that it spread no further among the people, let us strictly threaten them that they speak no more to anyone in this Name from now on."

So they called for Peter and John and commanded them not to speak at all nor teach in the Name of Jesus.

But Peter and John answered, "You judge whether it is right in the sight of God to listen to you more than to God. For we cannot but speak the things which we have seen and heard."

The rulers threatened them more, but then they let them go because they could find nothing for which to punish them. It would indeed be strange to punish someone for making a lame man well! The man who had been healed was more than forty years old, and the people glorified God because of this healing that had been done.

Being let go, Peter and John went to their own company and reported all that the chief priests and elders had said to them. When the believers heard it, they all had prayer together. "Lord, You are God," they said. "You made heaven, and earth, and all that is in them. You spoke through your servant David, saying, 'Why do the heathen rage, and the people imagine vain things?' For indeed, against Jesus did Herod, Pontius Pilate, the Gentiles, and the Jews all gather together. And now, Lord, see their threatenings, and grant us boldness to speak Your Word. Reach out Your hand to heal, and do many signs and wonders through the Name of Jesus."

When they had prayed, the place where they were gathered together was shaken. The believers were all filled with the Holy Ghost, and they spoke the Word of God with boldness.

Ananias and Sapphira

Acts 4:32–5:42

With great power the apostles gave witness of the resurrection of Jesus, and great grace was upon all the believers.

The multitude of people who believed were filled with love for God and for one another. They did not say that any of the things that belonged to them were their own, but they willingly shared their things with one another. And no one lacked anything, because those who owned land and houses sold them, brought in the money, and laid it down at the apostles' feet. Then the money was given to the people according to each of their needs.

One man who did this was a Levite from the country of Cyprus. The apostles had named him Barnabas, which means "son of consolation." This man sold his land and laid the money at the apostles' feet.

But there was another man named Ananias, who with his wife Sapphira sold a piece of land that they owned. They agreed together that they would keep back part of the money for themselves, but would pretend they were giving it all.

So Ananias brought part of the money and laid it down at the apostles' feet. But Peter was filled with the

Holy Spirit, and the Spirit told him that Ananias was not honest. Peter said, "Ananias, why has Satan filled your heart to lie to the Holy Ghost and to keep back part of the price of the land? While you had it, was it not your own? And after you sold it, could you not do with it what you wanted? Why have you planned this thing in your heart? You have not lied to men, but to God."

When Ananias heard these words, he fell down and died. This caused great fear to come on the people who heard what had happened.

The young men arose, wrapped up Ananias, carried him out, and buried him. His wife did not know what had happened.

About three hours later, his wife Sapphira came in. Peter said to her, "Tell me whether you sold the land for so much."

She said, "Yes, for so much."

Peter said to her, "How is it that you and your husband have agreed together to tempt the Spirit of the Lord? Behold, the feet of those who have buried your husband are at the door, and those men will also carry you out."

Immediately Sapphira fell down and died. When the young men came in and found her dead, they took her out and buried her beside her husband. As a result, great fear came upon all the church and upon as many as heard these things.

The apostles did many other signs and wonders among the people. Sick ones were brought out into the streets and laid on beds and couches, so that the shadow of Peter would fall on some of them as he passed by. There also came to Jerusalem a multitude out of the cities all around, bringing sick folks and those who were troubled with unclean spirits; and they were all healed. More and more believers were added to the church—both men and women.

All these things angered the high priest and the Sadducees who were with him. They rose up and arrested the apostles and put them into the common prison. But during the night, the angel of the Lord opened the prison doors and brought them out. "Go, stand in the temple," said the angel, "and speak to the people all the words of this life."

When the apostles heard that, they entered into the temple early in the morning and began teaching the people.

That morning the high priest and the men with him came and called the council together. Then they sent officers to the prison to get the apostles and bring them in for a trial.

The officers came to the prison, but they could not find the apostles. They returned and said, "The prison we truly found shut with all safety. The keepers were standing outside in front of the doors; but when we opened the doors, we found no one inside."

When the high priest and the rest of the council heard these things, they began to wonder how far this thing would go. Then someone came and told them,

"Behold, the men whom you put into prison are standing in the temple and teaching the people."

So the captain and officers went to the temple. For fear of the people, they brought the apostles back without force. When they stood before the council, the high priest asked them, "Did we not strictly command you that you should not teach in this Name? And now you have filled Jerusalem with your teaching, and intend to bring this Man's blood upon us."

Peter and the other apostles answered, "We ought to obey God rather than men. The God of our fathers raised up Jesus, whom you killed and hanged on a tree. Him has God raised up with His right hand to be a Prince and a Saviour in order to give repentance and forgiveness of sins to Israel. And we are His witnesses of these things, and so is also the Holy Ghost, whom God has given to those who obey Him."

These words cut the hearts of the rulers like a knife, and they began talking about putting the apostles to death. Then a Pharisee named Gamaliel stood up in the council. He was a teacher of the Law, and he was highly respected by the people.

Gamaliel gave orders that the apostles be put out of the room for a short time. Then he said, "You men of Israel, be careful what you do to these men. Some time ago Theudas rose up, boasting himself to be somebody, and about four hundred men joined themselves with him. But he was killed, and all the people who followed him were brought to nothing.

"After this man, Judas of Galilee rose up in the days of the taxing and drew many people after him. He also died, and all who obeyed him were scattered. Now I tell you, stay away from these men, and let them alone. For if their teaching and work is of men, it will come to nothing. But if it is of God, you will not be able to overthrow it; and you might even be fighting against God."

The other men agreed to what Gamaliel said. They called the apostles back in and gave them a severe beating. Again they commanded the apostles not to speak in the Name of Jesus, and then they let them go.

The apostles departed from the council, rejoicing that they were counted worthy to suffer shame for the Name of Jesus. And daily in the temple and from house to house they did not cease to teach and preach about Jesus Christ.

The Witness of Stephen

Acts 6:1–7:37

In those days there was a great increase in the number of believers. After a time the Greek-speaking Jews began to complain against the Hebrew-speaking Jews because their widows were neglected when daily supplies were distributed to the poor.

Then the twelve apostles called the believers together and said, "It is not reasonable that we should leave the Word of God and serve tables. We are not able to look after the daily needs of all these people. Therefore, brethren, find among you seven men who are reported to be honest and full of the Holy Ghost and wisdom, whom we may appoint over this work. But we will give ourselves continually to prayer and to the ministry of the Word."

These words pleased the whole multitude. They chose Stephen, Philip, Prochorus, Nicanor, Timon, Parmenas, and Nicolas, and these men were brought to the apostles. When they had prayed, the apostles laid their hands on them.

So the word of God increased, and the number of disciples continued to multiply in Jerusalem. Even a great company of the priests were obedient to the faith.

Stephen, a man full of faith and power and of the Holy Ghost, was doing great wonders and miracles among the people. Soon a group of men in the synagogue began disputing with him, but he spoke with such wisdom that they were not able to withstand his words. So they persuaded some men to say about Stephen, "We have heard him speak blasphemy against Moses and against God." In this way they stirred up the people against Stephen.

The elders and scribes caught Stephen and brought him to the council. They set up some men to tell lies about him. The false witnesses said, "This man does not stop speaking blasphemy against the holy place and against the Law. We have heard him say that this Jesus of Nazareth shall destroy this place and shall change the customs that Moses gave us."

When all the people in the council looked at Stephen, they saw that his face looked like the face of an angel.

Then the high priest asked Stephen, "Are these things so?"

Stephen began to speak. "Men, brethren, and fathers, listen. The God of glory appeared to our father Abraham when he was in Mesopotamia before he lived at Haran. God said to him, 'Get out of your country and from your relatives, and come into the land that I will show you.' So he came out of the land of the Chaldeans and lived at Haran. When his father was dead, he moved from there to this land where you now live.

"But God did not give him any inheritance in the

land, no, not even enough to set his foot on. Yet when he still had no child, God promised Abraham that He would give this land to him and to his family after him.

"God told Abraham that his descendants would stay for a time in a strange land. There they would be in slavery and would be treated unkindly four hundred years. But God would judge the nation that made them slaves, and He would bring them out of that land to serve Him in this land.

"Abraham had a son called Isaac, and Isaac had a son called Jacob. To Jacob were born twelve sons, called the twelve patriarchs.

"The patriarchs envied Joseph and sold him into Egypt, but God was with him. He delivered Joseph out of all his troubles and gave him favor and wisdom before Pharaoh, the king of Egypt. Pharaoh made him ruler over Egypt and all his house.

"Now there came a famine and great distress over all the earth, and our fathers could find no food. But when Jacob heard that there was food in Egypt, he sent our fathers there. The second time they went to Egypt, Joseph made himself known to his brothers, and Joseph's family was made known to Pharaoh.

"Then Joseph sent for his father Jacob to come down to Egypt to him, with all his sons and their families. At the time there were seventy-five people, including Joseph and his sons. So Jacob went down into Egypt and died, he as well as our fathers. Jacob was taken back and buried in the burying place that

Abraham had bought.

"But as the time of the promise drew near which God had promised Abraham, the people grew and multiplied in Egypt. Then there arose another king over Egypt, who did not know Joseph. This king was very cruel to our fathers and had their baby boys cast out so that they would not live.

"At this time Moses was born. He was a very lovely child and was cared for in his father's house for three months. And when he was cast out, Pharaoh's daughter took him and cared for him as her own son.

"Moses was taught in all the wisdom of the Egyptians and was mighty in words and deeds. When he was a full forty years old, it came into his heart to visit his brethren, the children of Israel. Seeing one of them suffer wrongfully, he defended him and killed an Egyptian. He thought his people should understand that God would use him to deliver them from slavery, but they did not understand. The next day he saw two men of Israel fighting together, and he tried to help them make peace with each other. 'Sirs, you are brethren,' he said. 'Why are you hurting one another?'

"But the man who was doing the wrong to his neighbor pushed Moses away. 'Who made you a ruler and judge over us?' he said. 'Do you mean to kill me as you did the Egyptian yesterday?'

"Then Moses ran for his life and was a stranger in the land of Midian. There he had two sons. When forty years had passed, the angel of the Lord appeared to

Moses in the wilderness of Mount Sinai in a flame of fire in a bush.

"When Moses saw it, he wondered at the sight and drew nearer to look at it. Then the voice of the Lord came to him, saying, 'I am the God of your fathers, the God of Abraham, the God of Isaac, and the God of Jacob.'

"Then Moses trembled and did not dare to look. The Lord said to him, 'Take off your shoes from your feet, for the place where you stand is holy ground. I have seen the trouble of My people who are in Egypt. I have heard their groaning and have come down to deliver them. Now come, I will send you into Egypt.'

"This Moses was refused with the words, 'Who made you a ruler and judge?' But God sent him to be a deliverer by the hand of the angel that appeared to him in the bush. He brought the people out after he had showed wonders and signs in the land of Egypt. He led them through the Red Sea and in the wilderness for forty years.

"This is the same Moses who said to the children of Israel, 'A Prophet like me shall the Lord your God raise up from your brethren. Him you shall hear.'"

Samaria Receives the Word of God

Acts 7:38–8:25

Stephen went on to tell the council the story of the children of Israel up to the time of King Solomon. Then he said, "You stiff-necked and unclean in heart and ears, you do always resist the Holy Ghost. As your fathers did, so do you. Which of the prophets have not your fathers persecuted? They killed the ones who foretold the coming of the Just One, whom you have now betrayed and murdered. You have received the Law, yet you do not even keep it yourselves."

When they heard these things, they were cut to the heart and gnashed on him with their teeth. But Stephen, being full of the Holy Ghost, kept looking up into heaven and saw the glory of God. "Look!" he said. "I see the heavens opened, and the Son of Man standing at the right hand of God."

This was too much for these men. They cried out with a loud voice, stopped their ears, and all together rushed upon Stephen. Then they drove him out of the city and began stoning him.

As they stoned him, Stephen called upon God, saying, "Lord Jesus, receive my spirit." He kneeled down and cried with a loud voice, "Lord, do not hold this sin against them." And soon after that he died.

The men who stoned Stephen had laid their clothes at the feet of a young man whose name was Saul. He was one of those who were in favor of having Stephen put to death.

Now a great persecution arose against the church at Jerusalem. It was so severe that the believers were scattered throughout Judea and Samaria because of it. Only the apostles remained at Jerusalem.

Sincere and religious men carried Stephen to his burial and wept much over him.

As for Saul, he made a very great destruction in the church. He entered one house after another and arrested both men and women. The people who were scattered because of this persecution went everywhere, preaching the Word.

Then Philip (one of the seven deacons) went down to the city of Samaria and preached Christ to the people there. The people paid attention to the things he said because they heard and saw the miracles that he did. Unclean spirits, crying with a loud voice, came out of many who were possessed with them. Many who were lame or had palsy were healed, and there was great joy in that city.

Now in the city of Samaria there was a certain man called Simon, who before this time had used magic with the help of evil spirits. He did such amazing wonders that he made the people of Samaria believe he was a great person. All the people looked up to him and said,

"This man is the great power of God." They honored him because for a long time he had amazed them with his magic.

But then Philip came, preaching about the kingdom of God and the Name of Jesus Christ. Many believed Philip and were baptized, both men and women.

Then Simon himself also believed and was baptized. He stayed with Philip and marveled when he saw the miracles and signs that were done.

When the apostles at Jerusalem heard that Samaria had received the Word of God, they sent Peter and John to them. These two apostles came down and prayed for the people so that they might receive the Holy Ghost. For as yet the Samaritans had not received Him; they had been baptized only in the Name of the Lord Jesus. When Peter and John laid their hands on the people, they received the Holy Ghost.

When Simon saw that the Holy Ghost was given through the laying on of the apostles' hands, he offered them money. He said, "Give me also this power so that on whomever I lay hands, he may receive the Holy Ghost."

Peter said to Simon, "Your money perish with you because you have thought that the gift of God may be bought with money. You have no part or lot in this matter because your heart is not right in the sight of God. Repent of your wickedness and pray to God. Perhaps he will forgive the thoughts of your heart, for I see that you are in the gall of bitterness and in the bonds of sin."

Simon answered, "Pray to the Lord for me so that none of these things that you have spoken may happen to me."

Peter and John stayed in Samaria for a time and preached the Word of the Lord to the people. Then they returned to Jerusalem, preaching the Gospel in many Samaritan villages as they went.

Conversions of the Ethiopian and Saul

Acts 8:26–9:22

The angel of the Lord said to Philip, "Arise, and go toward the south to the way that goes down from Jerusalem to Gaza, which is desert." Then Philip arose and went.

A man from the country of Ethiopia was traveling along that road. This man had great power under Candace, queen of the Ethiopians, and he was in charge of her treasure. He had gone up to Jerusalem to worship and was now returning. As he rode along in his chariot, he was reading from the book of the prophet Isaiah.

The Spirit said to Philip, "Go near, and join yourself to this chariot."

Philip ran to the chariot and heard the man reading the prophet Isaiah. He said, "Do you understand what you are reading?"

The man from Ethiopia answered, "How can I unless someone helps me?" He invited Philip to come up into his chariot and sit with him.

The place where the man was reading was the fifty-third chapter of Isaiah where it says, "He was led as a sheep to the slaughter; and like a lamb dumb before his shearer, so opened he not his mouth. In his humiliation

his judgment was taken away: and who shall declare his generation? for his life is taken from the earth."

The man asked Philip, "Please tell me of whom the prophet is speaking. Is it of himself, or of some other man?"

Then Philip began at that Scripture and preached Jesus to him. As they went on their way, they came to some water. The man said, "See, here is water. What hinders me from being baptized?"

Philip answered, "If you believe with all your heart, you may."

He answered, "I believe that Jesus Christ is the Son of God." He commanded the chariot to stand still, and they both went down into the water. There Philip baptized the man from Ethiopia.

When they had come up out of the water, the Spirit of the Lord caught away Philip, and the other man saw him no more. The Ethiopian went on his way rejoicing.

Philip was found at Azotus. He passed through that city and preached in all the cities till he came to Caesarea.

Saul was still busy threatening and punishing the disciples of the Lord. He went to the high priest and asked for letters to present to the synagogues in Damascus. These letters would give him authority that if he found any believers there, whether men or women, he might bring them bound to Jerusalem.

As Saul was on his way and coming near Damascus, suddenly a very bright light from heaven shone round about him. Saul fell to the earth and heard a voice saying, "Saul, Saul, why do you persecute Me?"

Saul asked, "Who are You, Lord?"

The Lord said, "I am Jesus whom you are persecuting. It is hard for you to kick against the pricks."

Saul was trembling and greatly astonished. "Lord, what do You want me to do?" he asked.

The Lord said to him, "Arise, and go into the city, and it shall be told you what you must do."

The men who journeyed with Saul stood speechless. They heard a voice but did not see anyone.

Then Saul arose from the earth, but when he opened his eyes, he could not see. The men who journeyed with him led him by the hand and brought him into Damascus. For three days Saul was blind and neither ate nor drank.

There was at Damascus a certain disciple named Ananias. The Lord came to him in a vision and said, "Ananias."

He answered, "Behold, I am here, Lord."

"Arise," said the Lord, "and go to the street that is called Straight. Inquire in the house of Judas for one called Saul of Tarsus; for, behold, he is praying. He has seen a vision of a man named Ananias coming in and putting his hand on him so that he may receive his sight."

Then Ananias answered, "Lord, I have heard by many about this man and about how much evil he has done to Your saints at Jerusalem. And here he has authority from the chief priests to bind all who call on Your Name."

But the Lord said, "Go your way, for he is a chosen vessel to Me, to take My Name to the Gentiles, to kings, and to the children of Israel. I will show him how much he must suffer for My Name's sake."

Ananias went his way and entered into the house. Putting his hands on Saul, he said, "Brother Saul, the Lord, even Jesus, who appeared to you in the way as you came, has sent me that you may receive your sight and be filled with the Holy Ghost."

Immediately there fell from Saul's eyes something like scales. At the same moment he received his sight, and then he arose and was baptized.

When Saul had eaten, he was strengthened. Then Saul stayed with the disciples at Damascus for a time. He began to preach in the synagogues that Jesus is the Christ, the Son of God.

But all who heard him were amazed and said, "Is not this the one who destroyed those who called on this Name in Jerusalem? Did he not come here to bring them bound to the chief priests?"

But Saul increased the more in strength and perplexed the Jews who were living at Damascus, proving that Jesus is truly the Christ.

Gentiles Receive the Holy Ghost

Acts 9:23–10:48

After many days the Jews in Damascus made plans to get rid of Saul. They watched the gates day and night for a chance to kill him. Saul learned that they were watching for him.

Then the disciples took him by night and let him down over the wall in a basket. In this way Saul escaped safely from the city.

When Saul arrived at Jerusalem, he tried to join the disciples, but they were afraid of him. They did not believe that He was a disciple. But Barnabas received him and declared to the apostles how Saul had met the Lord on the road. He also told them how he had preached boldly at Damascus in the Name of Jesus.

Then Saul was accepted, and he moved about freely in Jerusalem, boldly preaching in the Name of the Lord Jesus. But the Greek-speaking Jews began disputing with him, and soon they were making plans to kill him. When the brethren knew this, they brought Saul down to Caesarea and sent him from there to Tarsus.

Then the churches in Judea, Samaria, and Galilee had a time of rest from the terrible persecution they had endured. They were instructed and encouraged in the faith. They walked in the fear of God and in the comfort of the Holy Ghost, and they increased in numbers.

As Peter passed through many places, he came down to the saints at Lydda. There he found a man named Aeneas who had been bedfast for eight years. He was sick with palsy. Peter said to him, "Aeneas, Jesus Christ makes you well. Arise and made your bed."

Immediately Aeneas arose. All the people of Lydda and Saron saw him and turned to the Lord.

A disciple named Dorcas lived at Joppa. This woman was full of good works and almsdeeds, but about this time she became sick and died. Her friends washed her body and put her in an upstairs room. Lydda was near Joppa, and the disciples had heard that Peter was there. So they sent two men to Peter, requesting that he come without delay.

When Peter arrived, they brought him into the upper room. All the widows stood around him, weeping and showing the garments Dorcas had made while she was still with them.

Peter sent them all out of the room. Then he kneeled down and prayed. Turning to the body, he said, "Dorcas, arise."

She opened her eyes, and when she saw Peter, she sat up. Giving her his hand, Peter lifted her up; and when he had called the saints and widows, he presented her alive.

This great event became known throughout all Joppa, and many believed in the Lord. Afterward Peter stayed at Joppa many days with a man named Simon, who was a tanner.

In Caesarea there was a man named Cornelius who was a centurion of the Italian band. He was a sincere, religious man who feared God. All the members in his home also feared God. He gave much money to poor people, and he prayed to God continually. One day around three o'clock in the afternoon, he saw an angel in a vision. The angel said, "Cornelius."

When Cornelius looked at the angel, he was afraid. "What is it, Lord?" he asked.

The angel said, "Your prayers and your alms have come as a reminder before God. Now send men to Joppa and call for Simon, whose last name is Peter. He is lodging with Simon, a tanner, whose house is by the seaside. He shall tell you what you need to do."

When the angel left, Cornelius called two of his household servants and a devout soldier who served him. He told them about the vision, and then he sent them to Joppa.

The next day, as the men approached the city, Peter went up on the housetop about noon to pray. He was very hungry and wanted to eat, but while the food was being prepared, he had a vision.

Peter saw the sky opened and a vessel descending to him. It was like a great sheet fastened at the four corners and let down to the earth. In it were all kinds of four-footed beasts of the earth, wild beasts, creeping things, and fowls of the air.

A voice spoke to Peter. "Rise, Peter. Kill and eat."

The Old Testament Law allowed the Jews to eat only certain kinds of animals. Other animals were called unclean, and the Jews were not allowed to eat them. So Peter did not think it would be right for him to kill and eat these animals. He said, "No, Lord, for I have never eaten anything common or unclean."

The voice spoke again. "What God has cleansed, you should not call common."

This was done three times, and then the vessel was drawn back into the sky. While Peter wondered about the meaning of the vision, the men who had been sent from Cornelius arrived. They had inquired where Simon's house was, and now they were at the gate asking whether Simon Peter was lodging there.

As Peter continued thinking about the vision, the Spirit of God spoke to him. "Behold, three men are looking for you. Arise, and get down and go with them. Do not have any doubts about this, because I have sent them."

Then Peter went down to the men who were sent by Cornelius. "I am the one you are seeking," he said. "What is the reason you have come?"

They answered, "Cornelius the centurion, a just man who fears God and is well spoken of among all the Jews, was directed by an angel to send for you. He wants you to come to his house so that he may hear what you have to tell him."

Then Peter invited them to come in and gave them

a place to lodge for the night. The next day Peter and some of the brethren from Joppa went away with the men. A day later they arrived at Caesarea, where they found Cornelius waiting for them. He had called together his relatives and close friends so that they, too, might hear what Peter had to say.

As Peter was coming in, Cornelius met him and fell down at his feet to worship him. But Peter lifted him up, saying, "Stand up. I am also a man." As he talked with Cornelius, he went in and found many people gathered together.

Peter said to them, "You know that it is against our law for a Jew to keep company with one of another nation. But God has showed me that I should not call any man common or unclean, so I came without objecting. Now I ask you, what is the reason that you have sent for me?"

Cornelius answered, "Four days ago when I was fasting and praying, a man in bright clothes stood before me. He said, 'Cornelius, your prayer is heard and your alms are held in remembrance in the sight of God. Send therefore to Joppa and call for Simon, whose last name is Peter. He is lodging by the seaside in the house of Simon, a tanner. When he comes, he shall speak to you.' So immediately I sent for you, and you have done well that you have come. Now we are all present to hear the things that God commands you to say."

Then Peter said, "Truly I see that God does not consider any person better than another, but in every nation, whoever fears God and does righteousness is accepted by Him." He went on to tell Cornelius and his friends about the Lord Jesus Christ and how He died and rose again. He told them that whoever believes in the Name of Jesus can have forgiveness of sin.

While Peter was still preaching, the Holy Ghost fell on those who heard the Word. They spoke in different languages, glorifying and praising God.

The Jewish people who were with Peter were astonished. They did not know that the Holy Ghost would also be poured out on the Gentiles.

Peter said, "Can anyone forbid water, that these should not be baptized who have received the Holy Ghost the same as we?" He commanded them to be baptized in the Name of the Lord. Then they begged Peter to stay with them a while, for they were hungry to know more of the Word of God.

Lesson 9

Peter's Release From Prison

Acts 11:1–12:17

The apostles and brethren in Judea heard that the Gentiles had also received the Word of God. When Peter came up to Jerusalem, the Jews disputed with him, saying, "You went in to men who were not Jews and ate with them."

But Peter repeated the story from the beginning, telling them everything that had happened. He said, "I was in the city of Joppa praying. While in a trance, I saw a vision. A certain vessel came down, like a great sheet let down from the sky by the four corners. When I looked at it, I saw four-footed beasts of the earth, wild beasts, creeping things, and fowls of the air. I heard a voice saying to me, 'Arise, Peter. Kill and eat.'

"But I said, 'No, Lord, for nothing common or unclean has ever entered my mouth.'

"But the voice answered me from heaven, saying, 'What God has cleansed, you should not call common.' This was done three times, and all were drawn up again into the sky. And, behold, immediately three men came to the house where I was. They had been sent from Caesarea for me. The Spirit told me to go with them without any doubts. Besides this, six brethren went along with me; and we entered the house of Cornelius.

"He told us how he had seen an angel which said to him, 'Send men to Joppa and call for Simon whose last name is Peter. He shall tell you how you and all your house may be saved.'

"As I began to speak, the Holy Ghost fell on them the same as on us at the beginning. Then I remembered the Word of the Lord, how He said, 'John indeed baptized with water, but you shall be baptized with the Holy Ghost.' Since God gave them the same gift as He did to us who believed on the Lord Jesus Christ, who was I, that I could oppose God?"

When the Jews heard this, they were satisfied. They glorified God, saying, "Then God has also given to the Gentiles repentance to life."

Many believers were scattered after the persecution that arose because of Stephen. They traveled as far as Phoenicia, Cyprus, and Antioch, preaching the Word to the Jews. The Lord was with them and blessed their ministry. At Antioch a great number of Greek-speaking Jews believed and turned to the Lord.

When this news came back to the church at Jerusalem, they sent Barnabas to go to Antioch. When he came, he was glad to see how the grace of God was working among them. He urged them all that with determination they should live close to the Lord. Barnabas was a good man and full of the Holy Ghost and faith, and many people were added to the Lord.

Then Barnabas went to Tarsus to look for Saul.

When he found him, he brought him to Antioch. For a whole year Barnabas and Saul stayed with the church at Antioch and taught the people. It was there that the followers of Christ were first called Christians.

Some prophets also came to Antioch from Jerusalem. One of them, named Agabus, stood up and said by the Spirit that there would be a great famine throughout all the world. This famine came in the days of Claudius Caesar. Then the believers decided to send relief to the brethren who lived in Judea. They sent it to the elders with Barnabas and Saul.

About that time King Herod stretched forth his hands to persecute the church. He killed James the brother of John with the sword. Because he saw that this pleased the Jews, he arrested Peter also. Herod assigned sixteen soldiers to keep him, intending to bring him out to the people after the Passover.

So Peter was kept in prison, but the church prayed for him without ceasing.

The night before Herod was going to bring Peter out, probably to kill him, Peter was sleeping between two soldiers. He was fastened with two chains, and there were keepers in front of the door to keep watch. Then, behold, an angel of the Lord came upon him and a light shone in the prison. The angel hit Peter on the side and raised him up, saying, "Rise up quickly."

The chains fell off Peter's hands, and the angel said to him, "Put on your clothing and your sandals." Peter did this. The angel said, "Wrap your cloak around yourself and follow me." Peter went out and followed him, not realizing that what was being done by the angel was true. He thought he was seeing a vision.

They passed by the first and the second guard, and then they came to the iron gate that led to the city. This gate opened for them of its own accord, and they went out and walked along one street. Then suddenly the angel departed from him.

When Peter came to himself, he knew that this was not a vision but a real happening. He said, "Now I know for sure that the Lord did send His angel. He has delivered me out of the hand of Herod and from what the Jews were expecting to happen."

When he realized this, he went to the house of Mary the mother of John Mark, where many believers were gathered together praying. Peter knocked at the door of the gate, and a girl named Rhoda came to see who was there. When she recognized Peter's voice, she was so happy that she forgot to open the gate. She ran in and told them that Peter was standing outside the gate.

They said to her, "You are beside yourself."

But she insisted that it was true. Then they said, "It is his angel."

But Peter continued knocking. When they finally opened the gate and saw him, they were greatly astonished. He beckoned for them to be quiet; then he told them how the Lord had brought him out of the prison. He said, "Go tell these things to James and to the brethren." Then Peter left and went to another place.

Lesson 10

Paul and Barnabas as Missionaries

Acts 12:18–13:43

As soon as it was day, there was a great stir among the soldiers to know what had become of Peter. It was a serious thing for them to let a prisoner escape. When Herod looked for Peter and could not find him, he examined the keepers and commanded that they be put to death. Then Herod went down from Judea to Caesarea for a time.

Many people from Tyre and Sidon came to Herod while he was at Caesarea. Herod had earlier been displeased with them, but they desired to be at peace. Upon a set day Herod put on his royal apparel, sat upon his throne, and made a speech to them.

When the people heard it, they shouted, "It is the voice of a god and not of a man."

Immediately the angel of the Lord struck Herod because he did not give God the glory. Worms ate him and he died.

But the Word of God grew and multiplied. When Barnabas and Saul had finished their work at Jerusalem, they returned to Antioch, taking John Mark with them.

There were a number of prophets and teachers in

140

the church at Antioch. As they ministered to the Lord and fasted, the Holy Ghost said, "Separate to Me Barnabas and Saul for the work to which I have called them." So when they had fasted and prayed, they laid their hands on the two men and sent them away. John Mark also went along to help them.

Barnabas and Saul departed to Seleucia, and from there they sailed to the island of Cyprus. After they had preached the Word of God in the Jewish synagogues at Salamis, they went through the island to Paphos. Here they met a man who, like Simon in Samaria, did magic through the power of evil spirits. He was a Jewish false prophet named Bar-jesus, but he was also called Elymas the sorcerer.

Elymas was with Sergius Paulus, the deputy of the country. Sergius Paulus called for Barnabas and Saul, desiring to hear the Word of God. But Elymas withstood them, trying to turn the deputy away from the faith.

Then Saul (who was also known as Paul), filled with the Holy Ghost, looked at Elymas and sternly rebuked him. "O full of all subtlety and mischief, child of the devil, enemy of all righteousness," said Paul. "Will you not stop trying to turn others from the right ways of the Lord? Behold, the hand of the Lord is upon you, and you shall be blind for a time. You will not even be able to see the sun."

Immediately a mist of darkness fell upon Elymas, and he sought someone to lead him by the hand. And when the deputy saw what was done, he believed, being astonished at the doctrine of the Lord.

Soon afterward Paul and his group left Paphos and went to Perga in Pamphylia. John Mark left them there and returned to Jerusalem.

Paul and his group went on from Perga to another city called Antioch. It was called Antioch in Pisidia, whereas the city from which they had been sent was called Antioch in Syria. They went into the synagogue on the Sabbath Day and sat down. After the reading of the Law and the Prophets, the rulers of the synagogue said to Paul and Barnabas, "Men and brethren, if you have any word of advice or warning, say on."

Then Paul stood up, and beckoning with his hand he said, "Men of Israel and you who fear God, listen to us. The God of Israel chose our fathers and honored them when they lived as strangers in Egypt. With a great deliverance He brought them out, and for about forty years He put up with their ways in the wilderness. He destroyed seven nations in the land of Canaan and divided their land to Israel by lot. After that, for about four hundred fifty years, He gave them judges until Samuel the prophet.

"Then they wanted a king, and God gave them Saul the son of Kish, a man of the tribe of Benjamin. He was king for about forty years. After God removed him, He raised up David to be their king. Concerning David He said, 'I have found David, the son of Jesse, to be a man after My own heart, who shall bring to pass all My will.'

142

Of David's seed, according to His promise, God has raised a Saviour, Jesus. He came after John, who preached the baptism of repentance to all the people of Israel.

"As John was doing his work, he said 'Who do you think I am? I am not the Christ. But One is coming after me, whose shoes I am not worthy to loosen.'

"Men and brethren, children of Abraham, and whoever among you fears God, to you is the word of this salvation sent. The people of Jerusalem and their rulers, because they did not know the Lord nor the voices of the prophets, have done what the Scriptures said would happen. They condemned Jesus. Though they found no reason that He should die, yet they asked Pilate to have Him killed. And when they had done all that was written about Him, they took Him down from the tree and laid Him in a sepulcher.

"But God raised Him from the dead. He was seen many days by those who came up with Him from Galilee to Jerusalem, and they are His witnesses to the people. Now we declare to you the glad tidings that God has brought to pass the promise which He made to our fathers, in that He has raised Jesus up again.

"As for the fact that He rose from the dead, it is written in one of the Psalms, 'You will not allow Your Holy One to decay.' Now after David had served the people of his time, he died and was buried, and his body did decay. But He whom God raised again did not decay.

"So let it be known to you, men and brethren, that

through this Man the forgiveness of sins is preached to you. All who believe in Him are justified in the sight of God more than by the Law of Moses.

"Therefore beware lest it happen to you as the prophets said: 'Behold, you despisers, and wonder, and die. For I will do a work in your days that you will not believe, though a man declare it to you.'"

After the Jews left the synagogue, the Gentiles asked that those things be preached to them the next Sabbath Day. And when the congregation was scattered, many of the Jews and converted Gentiles followed Paul and Barnabas, who spoke to them and encouraged them to continue in the grace of God.

Paul and Barnabas Continue Their Ministry

Acts 13:44–14:3

On the next Sabbath Day, almost everyone in the city of Antioch came together to hear the Word of God. When the Jews saw the multitudes of people, they were filled with envy. People had never crowded around them like this. They began to contradict the things Paul said.

Then Paul and Barnabas became bold and said, "It was necessary that the Word of God should be spoken to you first. But seeing that you do not want it and you count yourselves unworthy of everlasting life, lo, we turn to the Gentiles. For the Lord commanded us, saying, 'I have set you to be a light to the Gentiles, for salvation to the ends of the earth.'" God had appointed Paul to take the Gospel to the Gentiles.

When the Gentiles heard this, they were glad. They praised and honored the Word of the Lord, and many believed. Soon the Word of God was published throughout all that region. But the Jews stirred up the devout and honorable women and the chief men of the city. They brought persecution against Paul and Barnabas and forced them to leave.

Paul and Barnabas shook the dust off their feet against them and left Antioch. But the disciples were filled with joy and with the Holy Ghost.

Paul and Barnabas traveled to Iconium next. There they went into the synagogue of the Jews and spoke to the people. A great multitude of both Jews and Greeks believed.

But the unbelieving Jews stirred up the Gentiles and caused them to think evil of the brethren. For a long time Paul and Barnabas stayed at this place, speaking boldly for the Lord. The Lord showed that He was speaking through them by allowing them to work signs and wonders.

But the multitude of the city was divided. Some believed the Jews and some believed what the apostles taught. Then the Jews and their rulers joined with the Gentiles and tried to harm the apostles and stone them. But Paul and Barnabas became aware of it and fled to Lystra and Derbe, other cities of Lycaonia. They preached the Gospel there and in the country around these cities.

At Lystra they saw a man who had been a cripple ever since he was born. He had never walked. As the crippled man listen to the Word, Paul watched him closely and knew he had faith to be healed. He said to him in a loud voice, "Stand up on your feet." And the man leaped up and began to walk.

When the people saw what Paul had done, they said in the language of Lycaonia, "The gods have come to us in the likeness of men." They called Barnabas Jupiter (father of the gods), and they called Paul Mercury (the god of oratory), because he was the main speaker. Then the priest of Jupiter brought oxen and wreaths to the city gates. The people were going to offer sacrifices to Barnabas and Paul!

When the apostles realized what was happening, they tore their clothes and ran in among the people. "Sirs, why do you do these things?" they cried. "We are also men such as you are. We preach to you that you should turn from these worthless gods to the living God who made heaven, earth, the sea, and all things in them. In times past God allowed all nations to walk in their own ways. But He gave witness of Himself by giving us rain from heaven and fruitful seasons, filling our hearts with food and gladness."

Even with these words they still could hardly keep the people from offering sacrifices to them.

Then some of the Jews from Antioch and Iconium came to Lystra. They persuaded the people against Paul. The multitude stoned Paul and then drew him out of the city, thinking he was dead. But while the disciples stood around him, he rose up and went back into the city.

The next day Paul and Barnabas left for Derbe, where they preached the Gospel and taught many people. Then they went back to Lystra, Iconium, and Antioch, strengthening the souls of the disciples and urging them to continue in the faith. They encouraged the believers by saying, "Through much tribulation we must enter the kingdom of God." They ordained elders in every church, and with prayer and fasting they committed the saints to the Lord to keep them.

Then they passed throughout Pisidia and came again to Pamphylia. When they had preached the Word in Perga, they went down to Attalia. From there they sailed back to Antioch in Syria, where they had been called to begin this work.

When they returned, they gathered the church together and rehearsed all that God had done for them. They also told how God had opened the door of faith to the Gentiles. For a long time they stayed with the disciples at Antioch.

Then certain men came from Judea to Antioch and taught the brethren that unless they were circumcised as Moses commanded, they could not be saved. In the Old Testament times, if a Gentile wanted to worship the God of the Jews, he had to become a Jew and be circumcised. But God had plainly showed Peter that this was no longer necessary. Both Jew and Gentile are alike to Christ. All are saved by faith and not by keeping the Law of Moses.

Paul and Barnabas talked much with these men from Judea, trying to help them see that they were wrong. Finally it was decided that Paul and Barnabas and certain other men should go up to Jerusalem to the apostles and elders to settle this question.

The church sent them out. On the way they passed

through Phoenicia and Samaria, and they told the brethren there about the conversion of the Gentiles. They caused much joy to all the brethren.

The Meeting at Jerusalem

Acts 15:4–16:8

When Paul and the men with him arrived at Jerusalem, they were received by the church and apostles and elders. They told the church all the things that God had done through them.

But some of the believing Pharisees said that it was necessary for the Gentiles to be circumcised and to keep the Law of Moses. The apostles and elders came together to consider this matter.

After there had been much discussion on the matter, Peter got up and said, "Men and brethren, you know that a good while ago God sent me to preach the Gospel to the Gentiles. He gave them the Holy Ghost even as He did to us, making no difference between us and them and purifying their hearts by faith. Now why do you try to put upon the neck of the disciples a yoke that neither our fathers nor we were able to bear? We believe that through the grace of the Lord Jesus Christ, we shall be saved, even as they."

Then the discussion ceased, and all the people listened as Paul and Barnabas told about the miracles and wonders which God had done among the Gentiles through them.

When they had finished, James said, "Men and brethren, listen to me. Peter has declared how God visited the Gentiles to take out of them a people for His name. The words of the prophets also agree with this. Therefore, my advice is that we do not trouble the Gentiles who have turned to God. But let us write to them, directing them to keep away from the filthiness of idols, from fornication, from things strangled, and from blood. For if they want to know the Law of Moses, they can hear it every Sabbath Day because it is read in all the synagogues."

Then it pleased the apostles and elders with the whole church to choose men from their own group and send them to Antioch with Paul and Barnabas. Judas and Silas, chief men among the brethren, were the ones chosen to go. The apostles also sent letters with them in which they wrote as follows:

From the apostles and elders and brethren, to the brethren who are of the Gentiles in Antioch and Syria and Cilicia, greetings.

We have heard that certain men went from us to you and troubled you, causing you to doubt your salvation by saying that you must be circumcised and keep the Law. But we gave them no such commandment. Now it seems good to us, being together in agreement, to send to you chosen men with our beloved Barnabas and Paul, who have risked their lives for the Name of our Lord Jesus Christ. Therefore we have sent Judas and Silas, who also shall tell you the same things. For it seemed good to the Holy Ghost, and to us, to lay upon you no greater burden than these necessary things: that you keep from eating meat offered to idols, from eating blood, from eating things strangled, and from fornication. If you keep yourselves from these things, you shall do well.

Farewell.

When the Gentiles read this letter, they rejoiced because of the comfort it gave them. Judas and Silas, who also were prophets, taught the people and strengthened them. After staying a while, they returned in peace to the apostles (though Silas decided to stay there longer). Paul and Barnabas also stayed at Antioch, teaching and preaching the Word of the Lord with many others as well.

After some time Paul said to Barnabas, "Let us go and visit our brethren in all the cities where we have preached, and see how they are getting along."

Barnabas wanted to take John Mark with them, but Paul disagreed. John Mark had left them at Perga in Pamphylia the last time. He had not gone along for the whole journey.

Barnabas felt so strongly that John Mark should go along, and Paul felt so sure that he should not go, that the two men separated. Barnabas took John Mark with him and sailed to Cyprus. Paul chose Silas to go along with him, being advised by the brethren that Silas was a good choice for this work. They went through Syria and Cilicia, strengthening the churches.

After this Paul came to Derbe and Lystra, where they met a certain disciple named Timothy. His mother was a Jewess who believed, but his father was a Greek. The brethren at Lystra and Iconium spoke very well of Timothy. Paul wanted Timothy to go along with him, which he did. As they went through the cities, they gave the believers the commands to keep which the apostles and elders at Jerusalem had decided upon. So the churches were strengthened in the faith and increased in numbers every day.

After they had gone through Phrygia and the region of Galatia, the Holy Ghost told them not to preach the Word in Asia. Then they came to Mysia, intending to go into Bithynia, but the Spirit would not allow them to go there. So they passed by Mysia and came down to Troas.

The Philippian Jailer

Acts 16:9–17:10

Paul had a vision that night at Troas. In his vision he saw a man from Macedonia who stood and begged, "Come over into Macedonia and help us."

So they immediately prepared to go into Macedonia, convinced that the Lord had called them to preach the Gospel there. From Troas they sailed toward Samothracia for a day, and then to Neapolis. From there they went to Philippi, a Roman colony which was the main city in that part of Macedonia.

The following Sabbath Day they went to the riverside outside the city, where it was customary for the women to meet for prayer. Paul and Silas sat down and talked to those who had gathered. There they met Lydia, a woman from the city of Thyatira. She was a seller of purple and one who worshiped God. When she heard the things Paul said, the Lord opened her heart, and she and her household were baptized.

Lydia begged Paul and Silas, saying, "If you have judged me to be faithful to the Lord, come into my house and stay there." And she would not be satisfied until they did.

As they went to prayer, a certain girl met them. She

was possessed with a spirit of divination and could tell things that were going to happen in the future. By making such predictions, she earned much money for her masters. The girl followed Paul and his companions, crying out, "These men are the servants of the most high God, and they show us the way of salvation."

The girl did this for many days, but it grieved Paul. Finally he turned and said to the spirit that possessed her, "I command you in the Name of Jesus Christ to come out of her." The spirit came out of her that very moment.

The girl's masters did not like this. Since the girl no longer had the spirit of divination, their hope of making money from her was gone. They caught Paul and Silas and brought them before the magistrates in the marketplace. The magistrates had authority to judge and to punish people. The girl's masters said, "These men, being Jews, do exceedingly trouble our city. They teach customs that are not lawful for us as Romans to keep."

This stirred up the people, and the multitude rose up together against the apostles. The magistrates tore their clothes off them and commanded that they be beaten. Paul and Silas received many lashes from whips and then were thrown into prison. The jailer was commanded to keep them safely, so he put them into the inner prison and made their feet fast in the stocks.

But Paul and Silas were not discouraged. At midnight they prayed and sang praises to God, and the other prisoners heard them. Suddenly there was a great earthquake which shook the foundations of the prison. All the prison doors were opened and all the prisoners' shackles were loosened.

The jailer awoke and saw that the prison doors were open. Immediately he drew his sword and was about to kill himself, for he supposed that all the prisoners had fled. But Paul called out loudly, "Do yourself no harm, for we are all here."

Then the jailer called for a light. He sprang into the inner prison and fell down trembling before Paul and Silas. He brought them out and asked, "Sirs, what must I do to be saved?"

"Believe on the Lord Jesus Christ, and you and your household shall be saved," they answered. Then they spoke the Word of the Lord to him and his household.

The jailer took them that same hour of the night and washed the wounds they had received from the whipping. Then he and all his house were baptized. When the jailer had brought them into his house, he set food before them and rejoiced, believing in God with all his household.

The next morning the magistrates sent word that these men should be let go. The keeper of the prison said to Paul, "The magistrates have sent word to release you. So you may depart in peace."

But Paul said, "We are Romans, and they have beaten us openly without a trial and have cast us into prison. Now do they intend to release us secretly? No, indeed; let them come themselves and bring us out."

When the magistrates heard that these men were Romans, they were afraid. Every Roman had the right to a trial before being punished. The magistrates could get in trouble if the Roman government found out what they had done. So the magistrates came and apologized. They brought Paul and Silas out of prison and begged them to leave the city.

Paul and Silas went to Lydia's house. After some fellowship with the brethren, they departed from Philippi.

When they had passed through Amphipolis and Apollonia, they came to Thessalonica. Paul went to the Jewish synagogue as usual. For three Sabbath Days, he tried to convince the Jews from the Scriptures that Jesus is the Christ. He explained that it was necessary for Christ to suffer and rise from the dead.

Some of them believed and joined the company of Paul and Silas. There were also a great multitude of sincere Gentiles and some chief women who believed. But the Jews who did not believe became envious. They gathered a crowd of wicked men from the lower class and set the city in an uproar. Then they attacked the house of Jason, where Paul and Silas were staying. But they could not find Paul and Silas, so they brought Jason and some other brethren before the rulers of the city. "These men who have turned the world upside down have come here also, and Jason has received them," declared the Jews. "They all contradict the laws of Caesar, saying there is another King, Jesus."

The people and the rulers were disturbed when they heard these things. But they let Jason and the other brethren go.

The brethren immediately sent Paul and Silas away to Berea in the night. When Paul and Silas arrived in Berea, they went into the synagogue of the Jews there.

Paul Preaches on Mars' Hill

Acts 17:11–18:11

The Jews in Berea were more noble than those in Thessalonica. They received the Word with ready minds, searching the Scriptures daily to see whether the things Paul and Silas said were true. As a result, many of the Berean Jews believed. There were also a good number of honorable Gentile men and women who believed.

But when the Jews at Thessalonica learned that Paul was preaching at Berea, they came and stirred up the people there. Then some of the brethren escorted Paul away from Berea, as though they were going to the sea (though Silas and Timothy stayed at Berea). Paul's escorts brought him to Athens. Then Paul sent them back with a message for Silas and Timothy to come to him speedily.

While Paul waited at Athens for Silas and Timothy, his spirit was stirred when he saw all the idolatry in the city. He had discussions with the Jews in the synagogue, with the devout people, and with those he met daily in the market.

A group of men given to study and reasoning met Paul. Some of them remarked, "He seems to be one who

159

sets forth strange gods" —for they heard him talking about Jesus and the resurrection. They brought Paul to Mars' Hill and asked, "May we know about your new teaching? For you bring strange things to our ears. We want to know what these things mean."

All the people of Athens and the strangers there spent their time in telling and hearing some new thing. So now, of course, they were interested in hearing what Paul had to say.

Paul stood up in the middle of Mars' Hill and said, "You men of Athens, I perceive that you are very religious. For as I passed by and saw your worship, I found an altar with this writing: 'TO THE UNKNOWN GOD.' This God, whom you worship in ignorance, is the One I will tell you about.

"He is the God who made the world and all things in it. He is Lord of heaven and earth and does not live in temples made with hands, neither is He worshiped with men's hands. He gives to all people life and breath and all things. He has made of one blood all nations of men to live on all the face of the earth. He has made all men with a desire to seek the Lord, and He is not far from every one of us. For in Him we live and move and have our being.

"Certain of your own poets have said, 'For we are His offspring.' So then, since we are the offspring of God, we should not think the Godhead is like gold, silver, or stone that is carved by the art and imagination of man. God in times past overlooked this ignorance, but now

He commands all men everywhere to repent. For He has appointed a day in which He will judge the world in righteousness by Jesus, whom He has ordained. He gave proof of this fact by raising Jesus from the dead."

When they heard of the resurrection of the dead, some mocked Paul. Others said, "We will hear you again about this matter." So Paul departed from among them, but there were a few men and women who stayed with him and believed.

After these things Paul left Athens and came to Corinth. There he found a Jew named Aquila who had been born in Pontus but later lived in Italy. He and his wife Priscilla had recently come from Italy because Claudius Caesar had commanded all the Jews to leave Rome. Aquila and Priscilla were tentmakers. That was also Paul's occupation, so he stayed and worked with them.

Every Sabbath, Paul taught in the synagogue and tried to persuade the Jews and the Gentiles. After Silas and Timothy came from Macedonia, Paul became so burdened for the Jews that he began spending all his time urging them to believe that Jesus is the Christ.

But when the Jews opposed Paul's teaching and blasphemed, Paul shook out his clothes before them. "Your blood is upon your own heads," he said. "I am clean. From this time on, I will go to the Gentiles." Then Paul went to the house of a man named Justus. This man worshiped God, and his house joined the synagogue.

Crispus, the chief ruler of the synagogue, believed on the Lord along with everyone in his household. Many of the Corinthians who heard also believed and were baptized.

The Lord spoke to Paul in a night vision, saying, "Do not be afraid, but speak and do not keep still. I am with you and no one shall hurt you, for I have many people in this city." So Paul stayed at Corinth a year and six months, teaching the Word of God.

Disciples at Ephesus

Acts 18:12–19:21

Once while Paul was at Corinth, the Jews rose up against him and brought him before Gallio, the deputy. They accused him, saying, "This man persuades people to worship God contrary to the Law."

But before Paul could speak, Gallio answered, "If it were a matter of crime, O you Jews, there would be reason for me to get involved. But if it is a question about words and names and your own Law, you must take care of it yourselves. I will be no judge of such things."

Having said this, Gallio drove them all away. Then the Greeks took hold of Sosthenes, the chief ruler of the synagogue, and began beating him before the judgment seat. But the deputy did not pay any attention to them.

Paul stayed at Corinth a while longer. Then he took his leave of the brethren there, and he, Aquila, and Priscilla began sailing toward Syria. At Cenchrea Paul had his head shaved because of a vow. At Ephesus he left Aquila and Priscilla and went into the synagogue, and there he began reasoning with the Jews. They wanted him to stay longer, but Paul would not consent. He bade them farewell, saying, "I must by all means keep the feast that is coming at Jerusalem. But I will return to you, if it is God's will." Then Paul sailed from Ephesus.

Paul landed at Caesarea and then went up to greet the church at Jerusalem. From there he went down to Antioch. After spending some time there, he left and went through the country of Galatia and Phrygia, strengthening all the disciples.

About this time there came to Ephesus a certain Jew named Apollos, who had been born at Alexandria. He was a good speaker and knew the Scriptures well. This man began to teach boldly in the synagogue, but he knew only about the baptism of John. He was not teaching the full Gospel. When Aquila and Priscilla heard him, they took him aside and taught him the way of God more perfectly.

When Apollos wanted to go to Achaia (or Greece), the brethren wrote a letter urging the disciples there to receive him. Apollos came to Achaia and was a great help to the believers. He publicly showed by the Scriptures that Jesus is the Christ, and mightily convinced the Jews.

While Apollos was at Corinth, Paul arrived at Ephesus after visiting the churches in Galatia and Phrygia. He found there some disciples and asked them, "Have you received the Holy Ghost since you believed?"

"We have not so much as heard whether there is any Holy Ghost," they answered.

Paul asked, "To what then were you baptized?"

They answered, "To John's baptism."

Paul said, "John truly baptized with the baptism of repentance, telling the people they should believe on the One coming after him. That One is Christ Jesus."

When they heard this, they were baptized in the Name of the Lord Jesus. Then Paul laid his hands on them and they received the Holy Ghost. They spoke in different languages and prophesied. There were about twelve men in this group.

Paul went into the synagogue and began speaking boldly. For three months he taught, persuading the people to believe the truth about the kingdom of God. But many people hardened their hearts and refused to believe. They spoke evil of God's kingdom before the multitude. So Paul and the disciples separated from them, and for two years Paul taught daily in the school of Tyrannus. In this way all the people in Asia, both Jews and Gentiles, heard the Word of the Lord Jesus.

At this time God worked special miracles by the hands of Paul. When handkerchiefs or aprons from his body were taken to people who had diseases or evil spirits, the sick became well and the evil spirits departed.

Some vagabond Jews who worked magic decided to use the Name of Jesus to drive out evil spirits. They took a man who had an evil spirit and said, "We command you by Jesus whom Paul preaches."

The evil spirit answered, "Jesus I know, and Paul I

know, but who are you?" And the man possessed by the evil spirit leaped on them and overcame them so that they fled from the house naked and wounded. Those men were the seven sons of Sceva, who was a Jew and chief of the priests.

All the Jews and Greeks living at Ephesus heard about this. They all feared and magnified the Name of the Lord Jesus, and many came and confessed their sins. Also, many of those who used magic brought their books together and burned them in the sight of all the people. They counted the value of all these books and found that they were worth fifty thousand pieces of silver. So the Word of God increased and prevailed.

After these things, Paul planned to travel through Macedonia and Achaia, and then return to Jerusalem. He said, "After I have been there, I must also see Rome."

Lesson 16

The Uproar at Ephesus

Acts 19:22–20:15

Though Paul wanted to return to Macedonia, he did not go there immediately. Instead he sent two of his helpers, Timothy and Erastus, while he stayed in Asia a while longer.

About that time there was a great disturbance in Ephesus. A silversmith named Demetrius was worried because many people were turning away from idols and worshiping God. They were no longer buying the shrines that Demetrius and the other silversmiths made for the goddess Diana. If this kept happening, the silversmiths would lose a great deal of money.

Demetrius called together the silversmiths and said, "Sirs, you know that we make our living by this craft. But as you see and hear, not only at Ephesus but throughout most of Asia, this Paul has turned away many people. He has persuaded them that the things made with hands are not gods. So there is the danger not only that we will lose our business, but also that the temple of the great goddess Diana shall be despised and her magnificence destroyed. All Asia and the world worship her."

When the silversmiths heard this, they were filled

with anger and began crying out, "Great is Diana of the Ephesians!" They kept shouting this until the whole city was filled with confusion. The men caught Gaius and Aristarchus, Macedonians who traveled with Paul, and rushed together into the theater. Paul wanted to go in, too, but the disciples would not let him. Some of the officials of Asia who were Paul's friends also urged him not to venture into the theater.

The people in the theater were confused. Some shouted one thing and some shouted another. Most of the people did not even know why they had come together.

Then the Jews put Alexander forward. He beckoned with his hand and was going to speak to the multitude, but when they learned that he was a Jew, they would not listen. "Great is Diana of the Ephesians!" cried the mob. For about two hours they kept shouting, "Great is Diana of the Ephesians!"

Finally the town clerk quieted the people. He said, "You men of Ephesus, what man is there who does not know that the Ephesians worship the great goddess Diana and the image which fell down from Jupiter? Seeing then that these things cannot be denied, you ought to be quiet, and do nothing hastily.

"You have brought here these men who are not robbers of temples, neither do they speak disrespectfully of your goddess. Therefore if Demetrius and the craftsmen who are with him have a matter against any man, the courts are open and there are deputies. Let them bring their charges to them so that their questions may be taken care of in a lawful meeting. We are in danger of being called in question for today's uproar, and there is no good reason that we can give for this disorderly gathering." With these words the town clerk dismissed the assembly.

After the uproar had ceased, Paul called the disciples to him and embraced them. Then he left for Macedonia. He visited the churches there and taught them. When he arrived in Achaia, he stayed there three months.

When he was about to sail for Syria, the Jews were watching for him, so he decided to return through Macedonia. A number of disciples wanted to return to Asia with him. They sailed to Troas and waited for him there. They were Sopater from Berea, Aristarchus and Secundus from Thessalonica, Timothy and Gaius from Derbe, and Tychicus and Trophimus from Asia.

Paul and his companions sailed from Philippi after the days of unleavened bread and came to Troas in five days. Here they stayed seven days.

On the first day of the week when the disciples came together to break bread, Paul preached to them. He was ready to leave the next day, but he had so many things to say that he continued speaking to them until midnight. They were gathered in an upper room, and they had many lights burning.

A young man named Eutychus was sitting in a window. Because Paul was preaching so long, he fell into a deep sleep and tumbled down from the third loft.

He was taken up dead.

Paul went down, fell on him, and embraced him. He said, "Do not be troubled, for his life is in him."

Paul went back upstairs and broke bread, and they ate together. Again he talked a long time, even until daybreak, and then he left. The people were very much comforted that Eutychus was alive.

Paul wanted to travel by foot from Troas to Assos. His companions took a ship and sailed ahead of him. When he met them at Assos, they took him on board and came to Mitylene. From there they sailed by Chios. The next day they arrived at Samos and stayed at Trogyllium, and the day following they came to Miletus.

Paul's Address to the Ephesian Elders

Acts 20:16–21:26

Paul decided to pass by Ephesus because he was in a hurry to get to Jerusalem by Pentecost if possible. In order to speak with the elders of the Ephesian church, Paul sent for them from Miletus. When they came to him, he said, "You know from the time I first came to Asia how I have lived among you, serving the Lord with all humility. You know of the tears and trials which came to me because the Jews were watching for me. I have not kept back anything from you, but have taught all things publicly as well as personally, testifying to both Jews and Gentiles.

"Now I am going to Jerusalem bound in spirit. I do not know what will happen to me there, but everywhere I go, the Spirit indicates that bonds and afflictions await me. But this does not move me. I do not count my life dear to myself, so that I might finish my course with joy. You will not see me again. So today I testify to you that I am free from the blood of all men. I have declared to you all the Word of God.

"Therefore take heed to yourselves and to all the flock over which the Holy Ghost has made you overseers, to feed the church of God. For I know that

171

after I depart, grievous wolves shall enter in among you, not sparing the flock. Also from among your own people shall men arise, speaking wicked things to draw away followers after them. Be watchful, therefore, and remember the warnings I gave day and night with tears in the past three years.

4. "And now, brethren, I commend you to God and the Word of His grace. His Word is able to build you up and to give you an inheritance among all those who are sanctified. Labor to support the weak and to give. Follow the example I gave of working for the things I needed instead of depending on others for money and clothing. Remember that Jesus said, 'It is more blessed to give than to receive.' "

5. When Paul finished speaking, he kneeled down and prayed with them. They all wept with much distress. They fell on his neck and kissed him, sorrowing most of all because he said they would see him no more. Then they all went with him to the ship.

6. After Paul and his companions left Miletus, they sailed toward Coos and the next day to Rhodes and from there to Patara. There they found a ship that would be sailing to Phoenicia, so they boarded that ship and set out. They passed to the south of Cyprus and landed at Tyre where the ship was to unload its goods. They found disciples there, so they stayed seven days. These disciples, through the Spirit, warned Paul that he should not go up to Jerusalem.

7. When the seven days were ended, they left to be on

their way again. The believers with their families accompanied them to the shore outside the city. There they kneeled down and prayed together. Then they parted: Paul and his company by ship, and the disciples back to their homes.

8 The ship stopped at Ptolemais. They stayed one day for fellowship with the brethren there. Then Paul's company traveled to Caesarea, where they entered the house of Philip the evangelist. Philip was one of the seven men ordained to care for the widows. He had four daughters who prophesied.

9 While they were staying at Philip's house, a prophet named Agabus arrived from Judea. When he saw Paul, he took Paul's waistband and bound his own hands and feet. He said, "Thus says the Holy Ghost, 'In this way the Jews at Jerusalem shall bind the man who owns this waistband, and shall deliver him to the Gentiles.'"

10 When they heard that, Paul's friends and the disciples of Caesarea began pleading with him, begging him not to go up to Jerusalem.

11 Paul said, "What do you mean to weep and to break my heart? For I am ready not only to be bound, but also to die at Jerusalem for the Name of the Lord Jesus."

12 When they saw that they could not persuade Paul, they stopped begging and said, "The will of the Lord be done."

13 Then Paul and his company went on to Jerusalem. Some of the disciples from Caesarea went along also. They brought with them an old disciple named Mnason

from Cyprus, with whom they would lodge.

14 When they arrived at Jerusalem, the brethren received them gladly. The next day Paul and his group had a meeting with James and all the other elders. When Paul had greeted them, he told them in detail about the things God had done for the Gentiles through his ministry.

15 The elders glorified the Lord when they heard these things. To Paul they said, "You see, brother, how many thousands of Jews there are who believe and who are eager to keep the Law. But they have been told that you teach all the Jews among the Gentiles not to obey Moses, not to circumcise their children, and not to keep the other customs. So this is what we suggest that you do. We have four men who have taken a vow upon themselves. Join them in their observance to show that you keep the Jewish customs yourself.

"As for the Gentiles who believe, we are satisfied that they do not have to keep the Jewish customs. We have written to them the things they need to observe: that they keep themselves from things offered to idols, from blood, from things strangled, and from fornication."

Paul agreed to their plan and joined the men who had taken the vow. He purified himself with them, and the next day he went into the temple to keep the days of purification.

Paul's Address at Jerusalem

Acts 21:27–22:29

Before the seven days of purifying were ended, some Jews from Asia saw Paul in the temple. They stirred up all the people and caught Paul, crying out, "Men of Israel, help! This is the man who teaches everyone against the Jews and the Law and the temple. He has even brought Gentiles into the temple and has defiled this holy place." They said this because earlier they had seen Paul in the city with Trophimus, an Ephesian. They supposed that Paul had brought him into the temple as well.

When the people heard this, they rushed together in great excitement. They drew Paul out of the temple and closed the doors. They were about to kill him, but just then news came to the Roman chief captain that all Jerusalem was in an uproar. Immediately he took soldiers and centurions and hurried to the scene. When the people saw the chief captain and the soldiers, they stopped beating Paul.

The captain took Paul and had him bound with two chains. Then he demanded of the people who Paul was and what he had done. But some cried one thing and some another, and the chief captain could not understand anything at all. So he commanded that Paul be taken into the castle.

The multitude followed after, crying, "Away with him!" And the people became so violent that the soldiers had to carry Paul part of the way. As they were about to take him into the castle, Paul asked the chief captain, "May I speak to you?"

"Can you speak Greek?" asked the captain. "Are you not the Egyptian who made an uproar and led four thousand murderers into the wilderness?"

Paul said, "I am a Jew of Tarsus in Cilicia, a citizen of an important city. Will you let me speak to these people?"

When the chief captain gave him permission, Paul stood on the stairs and motioned with his hand to the people. Finally there was a great silence, and Paul began speaking to them in the Hebrew tongue. "Men, brethren, and fathers, listen to my defense, which I now make to you."

When the people heard that he spoke in Hebrew, they became even more quiet. Paul continued, "I am indeed a Jew born in Tarsus in Cilicia, yet brought up in this city at the feet of Gamaliel. I have been taught according to the Law of the fathers and am eager to obey God, as you all are today. I persecuted the believers to death, binding and arresting both men and women. The high priest and all the elders can witness to this. They gave me letters and sent me to Damascus to bind those who were there and bring them to

Jerusalem to be punished.

"As I was coming near Damascus about noon, suddenly there shone around me a great light from heaven. I fell to the ground and heard a voice saying to me, 'Saul, Saul, why do you persecute Me?' I answered, 'Who are You, Lord?' He said to me, 'I am Jesus of Nazareth, whom you are persecuting.' They who were with me saw the light but did not hear the voice that spoke to me. And I said, 'What shall I do, Lord?' He said to me, 'Arise, and go into Damascus, and there you will be told all the things that are appointed for you to do.'

"I could not see because of the glory of that great light. So the others with me led me by the hand, and I came into Damascus. Ananias, a godly man according to the Law, lived there. He came to me and said, 'Brother Saul, receive your sight,' and that same moment I could see. He said, 'The God of our fathers has chosen you to know His will and see the Just One and hear the voice of His mouth. For you shall be His witness to all men of what you have seen and heard. Now why do you wait? Arise and be baptized and wash away your sins, calling on the Name of the Lord.'

"And when I came back to Jerusalem and was praying in the temple, I fell into a trance. Then the Lord said to me, 'Hurry and get out of Jerusalem, for they will not receive your testimony about Me.'

"And I said, 'Lord, they know that I beat and imprisoned those who believed on You. When Stephen was stoned, I was standing by consenting to his death, and I kept the clothes of those who killed him.'

"But the Lord said, 'Depart, for I will send you far away to the Gentiles.'"

The people listened quietly up to this point. But as soon as Paul said the word *Gentiles*, the uproar started all over again. "Away with such a fellow from the earth!" the mob cried. "It is not fit that he should live!" The people became so violent that they began casting off their outer clothes and throwing dust into the air.

The chief captain commanded the soldiers to bring Paul into the castle and lash him with whips. He wanted to find out what Paul had done to make the crowd so furious. As they were binding him with leather straps, Paul said to the centurion who stood by, "Is it lawful for you to whip a Roman before he has had a trial?"

When the centurion heard that, he went to the chief captain and said, "Be careful what you do, for this man is a Roman."

Then the chief captain came and said to Paul, "Tell me, are you a Roman?"

"Yes," Paul answered.

The captain said, "I obtained this freedom with a great sum of money."

Paul said, "But I was born free."

Then immediately those who were going to whip Paul went away from him. The chief captain was also afraid because he had ordered Paul to be bound.

Paul Is Taken to Caesarea

Acts 22:30–23:35

The next day the chief captain called the Jewish council together. He released Paul from his bands and brought him before the council in order to find out why the Jews accused him.

Paul addressed the council, saying, "Men and brethren, I have lived in all good conscience before God until this day."

The high priest, Ananias, commanded those who were standing by Paul to slap him on the mouth.

Then Paul said to him, "God shall smite you, you whited wall. Do you sit to judge me according to the Law and then command me to be struck contrary to the Law?"

Those who stood by said, "Do you revile God's high priest?"

Then Paul said, "Brethren, I did not know that he was the high priest. The Law says that we are not to speak evil of the ruler of the people."

When Paul realized that part of the council were Sadducees and part were Pharisees, he cried out, "Men and brethren, I am a Pharisee, the son of a Pharisee. It is because of the hope and resurrection of the dead that

I am being examined."

This caused a sharp division in the council. The Sadducees did not believe in the resurrection of the dead, neither in angels or spirits. But the Pharisees believed in all of these.

A great cry arose among the Pharisees and Sadducees. The scribes on the side of the Pharisees cried out, "We do not find any evil in this man. If a spirit or an angel has spoken to him, let us not fight against God."

The struggle became so great that the chief captain was afraid they would pull Paul to pieces. He commanded the soldiers to take him by force from the council and bring him into the castle.

The following night the Lord stood by Paul and said, "Be of good cheer, Paul. For as you have testified of Me at Jerusalem, so you must also testify at Rome."

The next day more than forty Jews came together and bound themselves under an oath, saying that none of them would eat or drink until they had killed Paul. They came to the chief priests and elders and said, "We have bound ourselves under a great curse, that we will eat nothing until we have killed Paul. Now you ask the chief captain to bring Paul down to the council again tomorrow, as if you want to ask him more questions. We will be ready to kill him as he comes by."

But Paul's sister's son heard about this scheme. He went into the castle and told Paul. Then Paul called one of the centurions and said, "Take this young man to the chief captain, for he has something to tell him."

So the centurion brought Paul's nephew to the chief captain, saying, "Paul the prisoner asked me to bring this young man to you. He has something to say to you."

The chief captain took the young man by the hand and privately went aside with him. "What is it that you have to tell me?" he asked.

The young man said, "The Jews have agreed to ask you to bring Paul before the council again tomorrow, as if to ask him more questions. But do not grant their request because more than forty of them have bound themselves under an oath not to eat or drink until they have killed Paul. They will be waiting to kill him along the way."

The chief captain said, "Do not tell anyone that you have reported this to me." Then he dismissed the young man.

Then the chief captain called for two centurions. He said, "Get ready two hundred soldiers, seventy horsemen, and two hundred spearmen to go to Caesarea at nine o'clock this evening. Provide an animal for Paul to ride, and take him safely to Felix the governor."

The chief captain wrote a letter to send with them to the governor. This is what he wrote:

From Claudius Lysias to the most excellent governor Felix, greetings.

This man was arrested by the Jews, and they would have killed him. Then I came with an army and rescued him, having understood that he was a Roman. In order to find out why they accused him, I brought him before their council. I understood that they were accusing him of questions about their law, but nothing was done against him that made him worthy of death or bonds.

And when I was informed that the Jews were waiting to attack him, I immediately sent him to you. I have also commanded his accusers to come before you with their charges against him.

Farewell.

That night the soldiers escorted Paul to Antipatris. The next day the horsemen went on with Paul, and the other soldiers returned to the castle. When the band arrived at Caesarea, they delivered the prisoner and the letter to the governor. He read the letter and asked what province Paul was from. When he understood that he was from Cilicia, he said to Paul, "I will listen to you when your accusers come." He commanded Paul to be kept in Herod's judgment hall.

Paul Before Felix and Festus

Acts 24:1–25:12

Five days later, Ananias the high priest, the elders, and a certain orator named Tertullus arrived at Caesarea. When Paul was called out before them, Tertullus began to speak to Felix against Paul. He said, "Seeing that we enjoy great quietness and that very worthy deeds are done to our nation by your ruling, we accept it with gratitude, most noble Felix. I do not want to be tiresome to you, but I ask you to please listen to a few words. We have found this man a troublesome fellow who causes rebellion among the Jews throughout the world. He has even tried to defile the temple. We took him and would have judged him according to our law, but the chief captain Lysias came and took him out of our hands by force. He commanded Paul's accusers to come to you. If you ask them, they will testify to the truth of these things."

The Jews agreed that the things Tertullus said were true.

When the governor beckoned for Paul to speak, he answered, "Since you have been a judge of this nation for many years, I can very cheerfully answer for myself. You should know that only twelve days have passed since I went up to Jerusalem to worship. They found me in the temple neither disputing with any man, nor stirring up the people, either in the synagogues or in the city. Neither can they prove the things of which they now accuse me.

"But this I confess to you, that I do worship the God of my fathers in a way that they call heresy. I believe all the things written in the Law and in the prophets. I have hope toward God, which they believe also, that there shall be a resurrection of the dead, both of the just and the unjust. And I always work to have a clear conscience toward God and men.

"Now after many years, I came to bring alms and offerings to my nation. Then certain Jews from Asia found me purified in the temple without any multitude or riot. They ought to come before you and accuse me if they have anything against me. Or if the ones here found any evildoing in me while I stood before their council, let them say so—unless it would be what I cried out about the resurrection of the dead."

Felix knew something about the way Paul believed. When he heard Paul's defense, he put the people off by saying, "When Lysias the chief captain shall come down, I will know everything about the case."

Felix commanded a centurion to keep Paul. Paul was not to be bound, and he was not to be denied visits from his friends.

Several days later Felix came with his wife Drusilla, who was a Jewess. He sent for Paul and listened to him about his faith in Christ.

As Paul talked about righteousness, temperance, and the judgment to come, Felix trembled. "Go you way for this time," he said. "When I have a convenient time, I will call for you."

Felix also hoped that Paul would offer money to bribe Felix into releasing him. So he sent for Paul often and talked with him.

After two years Felix was replaced by Festus. And because Felix wanted to please the Jews, he left Paul in prison.

Three days after becoming governor, Festus left Caesarea and went up to Jerusalem. There the high priest and the chief men of the Jews informed him against Paul. They asked him to send for Paul to come to Jerusalem, intending to watch for him on the way and kill him.

But Festus told them that Paul should be kept at Caesarea and that he himself would soon go there. He said, "Let those among you who are able go along and accuse this man if there is any wickedness in him."

When he had stayed with them ten days or more, he returned to Caesarea. The next day he sat on the judgment seat and commanded that Paul be brought.

When Paul came, the Jews who had come with Festus from Jerusalem made terrible accusations which they could not prove. Paul answered, "I have done nothing against the Law of the Jews, nor against the temple, nor even against Caesar."

186

But Festus, willing to please the Jews, asked Paul, "Will you go up to Jerusalem to be judged of these things before me?"

Paul said, "I stand at Caesar's judgment seat, where I ought to be tried. You know that I have done no wrong against the Jews. If I have done anything worthy of death, I do not refuse to die. But if I am not guilty of the things they accuse me of, no one can turn me over to them. I appeal to Caesar."

Festus conferred with his council and then said to Paul, "Have you appealed to Caesar? To Caesar you shall go."

Lesson 21

Paul's Address to Agrippa

Acts 25:13–26:32

Some time later, King Agrippa and Bernice came to Caesarea to greet Festus. After they had been there many days, Festus told King Agrippa about Paul's case. He said, "There is a certain man who was left a prisoner by Felix. When I was at Jerusalem, the chief priests and the elders of the Jews told me about him and wanted him to be sentenced to death. I told them the Romans do not deliver a man to die before he has a chance to meet his accusers face to face and defend himself against their accusations.

"When they came here, I sat on the judgment seat and had the man brought out. But the accusers did not bring any charges such as I expected. Their charges had to do with their own religion and with one Jesus, who was dead but whom Paul declared to be alive. Because I did not know about this kind of questions, I asked him whether he would go to Jerusalem to be judged of these matters. But Paul appealed to Caesar, so I commanded him to be kept until I might send him to Caesar."

Agrippa said to Festus, "I would like to hear this man myself."

"Tomorrow," said Festus, "you shall hear him."

The next day Agrippa and Bernice came with great splendor. They entered the place of judgment with the chief captains and great men of the city. At the command of Festus, Paul was brought before them.

Festus said, "King Agrippa, and all men present here with us, you see this man whom the Jews say should be put to death. When I found that he had done nothing worthy of death and that he himself had appealed to Caesar, I determined to send him. But I have nothing definite to write to Caesar about him. So I have brought him before you especially, O King Agrippa, that after examination I might have something to write. For it seems unreasonable to send a prisoner and not tell of what crimes he is accused."

Then Agrippa said to Paul, "You are permitted to speak for yourself."

Paul stretched out his hand and began his address. "I am happy, King Agrippa, to answer for myself before you, because I know that you understand the customs and questions of the Jews. So I ask you to listen patiently to me.

"The Jews know my early life as a strict Pharisee. And now I am judged and accused for the hope of the promise that God made to our fathers. Why should it seem unbelievable to you that God should raise the dead? But I tried to do many things against Jesus and His followers. With permission from the chief priests I shut up many of the saints in prison, and when they were put to death, I testified against them. I persecuted them even to foreign cities. For this purpose I went to Damascus with permission and orders from the chief priests.

"As I went, at midday, O King, I saw a light from heaven, brighter than the sun, shining around me and my companions. We all fell to the earth, and I heard a voice speaking to me in Hebrew and saying, 'Saul, Saul, why do you persecute Me? It is hard for you to kick against the pricks.' And I said, 'Who are You, Lord?' He said, 'I am Jesus whom you are persecuting. But rise, and stand on your feet. I have appeared to you to ordain you as a witness of the things you have seen and of the things that will be revealed to you. I will deliver you from the people and from the Gentiles, to whom I am sending you. I will send you to open their eyes and to turn them from darkness to light and from the power of Satan to God. Then they also may receive forgiveness of sins and inheritance with those who are saved by faith in Me.'

"Therefore, O King Agrippa, I was not disobedient to the heavenly vision. I preached first to them of Damascus, Jerusalem, and all Judea, and then to the Gentiles, that they should repent and live lives that show repentance.

"That is why the Jews caught me in the temple and tried to kill me. But God helped me, and I am still here today, preaching nothing except what Moses and the prophets said would happen. They said that Christ would suffer, that He would be the first to rise from the dead, and that He would give light to the people and to the Gentiles."

While Paul was saying these things, Festus spoke up in a loud voice. "Paul, you are beside yourself. Much learning is making you crazy."

But Paul said, "I am not crazy, most noble Festus. I speak clearly the words of truth and soberness, and King Agrippa knows about these things. I am sure they are not hidden from him, because this was not done in a corner. King Agrippa, do you believe the prophets? I know that you believe."

Then Agrippa said to Paul, "In a short time you would persuade me to be a Christian."

Paul answered, "I wish before God that not only you, but everyone who hears me today were both almost and altogether as I am, except for these bonds."

When he had said this, the king, the governor, Bernice, and those who sat with him arose and went aside to talk among themselves. They said, "This man is not doing anything worthy of death or imprisonment."

Then Agrippa said to Festus, "This man might have been set free if he had not appealed to Caesar."

Shipwreck

Acts 27

When it was decided that Paul should sail to Italy, he and some other prisoners were delivered to a centurion named Julius, who was of Augustus' band. Luke and Aristarchus went with Paul. They entered a ship of Adramyttium and launched from Caesarea. Since Aristarchus was a Macedonian from Thessalonica, they intended to sail by the coast of Asia.

The next day they landed at Sidon. There Julius kindly gave Paul liberty to go to his friends and refresh himself.

When they had launched from Sidon, they sailed on the lee side of Cyprus. The winds were from the west, and the sea was calmer on the east and north side of the island. When they had sailed over the sea of Cilicia and Pamphylia, they came to Myra, a city of Lycia.

There the centurion found a ship of Alexandria sailing into Italy, and he transferred his prisoners into this ship. Then they sailed many days, but could not get to Cnidus because of the wind. So they sailed on the lee side of Crete by Salmone. They passed it with difficulty, and came to a place called Fair Havens, near the city of Lasea.

Much time had now been spent, and sailing was becoming dangerous because it was late in the season. Paul advised the men, saying, "Sirs, I see that this voyage will bring harm and damage, not only to the cargo and the ship, but also to our lives."

But the centurion believed the pilot and the owner of the ship more than Paul. Besides, the harbor was not a suitable place to spend the winter. Most of the people thought they should leave there and try to get to Phenice, where they could spend the winter in a harbor which faces the southwest and northwest. So when the south wind blew softly, they supposed they would be able to make the voyage to Phenice. They loosed from Fair Havens and began sailing close by Crete.

But soon after they started, a tempestuous wind rose against them. The ship was caught in the full force of the wind, and the sailors could only let themselves be driven along. Running by the lee side of the island Clauda, they had great trouble to secure the small boat towed by the ship. When they got the boat on board, they bound cables around the sides of the ship to strengthen it. Then fearing that they would run aground in a shallow part of the sea, they lowered the sail and were driven by the wind. The tempest continued to toss them, and the next day they threw some of the cargo overboard to lighten the ship. On the third day they threw out the equipment of the ship.

When the tempest continued many days without any appearance of the sun or stars, they gave up all hope that they should be saved. Then Paul stood up in their midst and said, "Sirs, you should have listened to me and stayed at Fair Havens and avoided this harm and loss. But be of good cheer, for no one among you shall lose his life, although the ship will be destroyed. The angel of God stood by me in the night, saying, 'Fear not, Paul; you must be brought before Caesar. And God has given you all those who sail with you.' So be of good cheer, sirs, for I believe God, that it shall be just as He said. However, we will be cast upon an island."

In the fourteenth night of the storm, they were driven up and down in the Adriatic Sea. About midnight the sailors realized they were drawing near land. They measured to see how deep the water was and found it to be one hundred twenty feet deep. When they had gone a little farther, they measured again and found it to be ninety feet deep. They were afraid they would be cast upon the rocks, so they dropped four anchors out of the stern and wished for daylight.

The sailors went to the front part of the ship, pretending to let down anchors from there, but they were really lowering the small boat in order to escape from the ship. Paul said to the centurion and the soldiers, "Unless these men stay in the ship, you cannot be saved." Then the soldiers cut the ropes of the boat and let it fall into the sea.

When the day was dawning, Paul encouraged everyone to eat. He said, "This is the fourteenth day that you have been fasting. So please take some food, for this is for your own health. There shall not a hair fall from the head of any of you." Then he took bread and gave thanks to God in the presence of them all. When he had broken it, he began to eat. Then the others were encouraged and also took some food. In all there were two hundred seventy-six people on the ship.

When they had eaten enough, they lightened the ship by throwing the wheat into the sea. And when full daylight came, they did not recognize the land where they were. But they discovered a bay with a shore, and they decided to steer the ship into the bay if possible. So they took up the anchors and loosened the rudder bands. Then they lifted up the mainsail to the wind and started toward the shore. But in a place where two seas met, they ran the ship aground. The front part of the ship stuck fast and could not be moved. The back part of the ship began to break up under the force of the waves.

The soldiers suggested killing the prisoners so that they would not swim out and escape. But Julius wanted to save Paul, so he kept them from doing this. He commanded that those who could swim should first jump overboard and get to land. Then the others should escape, some on boards and some on broken pieces of the ship. In this way they all came safely to land, just as Paul had said they would.

Paul at Rome

Acts 28

When all the people had escaped, they found that they were on the island of Melita. The natives of Melita were very kind to them. They started a fire and received everyone because it was cold and raining.

Paul gathered a bundle of sticks and laid them on the fire. As he did so, a poisonous snake came out of the heat and bit into his hand. Seeing the snake hanging on Paul's hand, the natives said among themselves, "No doubt this man is a murderer. Though he has escaped the sea, he is not supposed to live because of his sin."

Paul shook off the snake into the fire and felt no harm. The people watched him for a while, expecting him to swell or suddenly fall down dead. But after they watched a long time and saw that no harm came to him, they changed their minds and said he was a god.

The chief man of the island, named Publius, lived in that area. He received the people and lodged them courteously three days. Publius's father was sick with a fever and dysentery. Paul prayed for him and laid his hands on him, and the Lord healed him. After this, others who had diseases came and were healed.

For the three months of winter the shipwrecked

people stayed on the island of Melita. A ship of Alexandria had also spent the winter there. When that ship sailed, Paul and his companions went along. The natives showed them many honors when they left, and gave them supplies for their trip.

The ship landed at Syracuse and stayed three days. From there they followed the coast and came to Rhegium. After one day the south wind blew, and the next day they ended their voyage at Puteoli.

They found brethren at Puteoli and stayed with them seven days. Then they went on toward Rome. When the brethren in Rome heard of Paul's coming, they came to meet them as far as Appii Forum and the Three Taverns. Paul thanked God and took courage when he saw the brethren.

When they arrived at Rome, the centurion delivered the prisoners to the captain of the guard. But Paul was allowed to live by himself with a soldier who kept him.

After three days, Paul called the leading men of the Jews together. "Men and brethren," he said, "I have committed nothing against the people or against the Jewish customs, but I was delivered prisoner from Jerusalem into the hands of the Romans. They examined me and would have let me go, but the Jews spoke against it, so I appealed to Caesar. But I do not come with any accusation against the Jews. It is for the very hope of Israel that I am bound with this chain. And it is about that hope that I have called for you, to see you and speak with you."

The Jews answered, "We have not received letters from Judea about you, neither did the brethren who came indicate anything evil. But we want to hear what you think, for we know that this doctrine is everywhere spoken against."

So they appointed a day and many came to Paul's house to hear his message. From morning till evening he explained about the kingdom of God, trying to persuade them about Jesus both from the Law of Moses and from the prophets.

Some of them believed the things he said, and some did not believe. When they disagreed among themselves, Paul reminded them of a prophecy. He said, "The Holy Ghost has well spoken by the prophet Isaiah, saying, 'Go to this people and say, Hearing you shall hear and shall not comprehend, and seeing you shall see and not perceive. For the hearts of these people are insensitive, and their ears are dull of hearing, and their eyes have they closed; lest they should see with their eyes and hear with their ears and understand with their hearts and should be converted and healed.' Be it known to you therefore, that the salvation of God is sent to the Gentiles, and they will hear it."

When Paul had said this, the Jews left his house, and they had much discussion among themselves.

Paul lived two whole years in his rented house and welcomed all who came to him. He preached the Kingdom of God and taught about the Lord Jesus Christ with all confidence, no man hindering him.

Unit Three

Job, Psalms, Proverbs

Job's Affliction

Job 1:1–2:10

Long ago in the land of Uz there lived a man named Job. He was a perfectly upright man, for he feared God and carefully avoided everything that was evil. Job was a rich man. His possessions included seven thousand sheep, three thousand camels, five hundred yoke of oxen, and five hundred she asses. Job's household of servants was very great. He was the greatest of all the men in the East.

Job had a dear family of seven sons and three daughters. His sons often had feasts together. Each of the sons had the others come to his house on a certain day of the week. They also invited their sisters to share with them in their feasts.

Job was concerned about the souls of his children. When they feasted together, Job realized that they might be tempted to dishonor God in their hearts. So for the good of his children, Job offered sacrifices to God and prayed for each one.

There came a day when God's angels gathered before God. Satan came among them, too. God said to Satan, "Where do you come from?"

Satan answered, "From going back and forth in the

earth and from walking up and down in it."

"Have you considered my servant Job?" asked the Lord. "He is a perfectly upright man who fears God and avoids all evil."

Satan scoffed, "Does Job fear God for nothing? You have put a hedge around him and his house and all his things. You have made things go well for him and have made him rich. That is why he fears You. But if You should take his riches away, it would be different. He would curse You to Your face."

God told Satan, "I will let you have power over all that he has. Take it away from him if you want to and see what happens. But you are not allowed to do anything to Job himself."

Satan went away from the presence of the Lord and set about to destroy Job's riches. All in one day, Satan brought four disasters into Job's life.

On a day when Job's children were feasting at the oldest brother's house, a messenger came to Job with dreadful news. He reported, "We were plowing with the oxen, and the asses were grazing nearby, when the Sabeans fell upon us. They took the animals away and killed the servants with the sword. I am the only one who escaped to tell you."

While he was still speaking, one of the servants who took care of Job's sheep arrived. "Fire fell from heaven," he reported, "and it burned up all the sheep and the servants. I am the only one alive to tell you."

While this man was giving his message, a third

servant appeared. "The Chaldeans attacked us," he said, "They made three bands and fell upon the camels. They killed the servants and took all the camels away. I am the only one left alive to tell you."

While he was yet speaking, still another messenger came with the saddest news of all. "Your sons and daughters were eating and drinking at the oldest brother's house. A great wind came from the wilderness and hit the four corners of the house. The house fell and killed everyone in it. I am the only one who survived to tell you."

What a dark and terrible day that was for Job! He got up and tore his clothes and shaved his head. He fell down and worshiped God, saying, "I had nothing when I came into this world, and I can take nothing with me when I leave. The Lord gave, and the Lord has taken away. Blessed be the Name of the Lord." Job did not curse God to His face. He knew God is perfect and just, and he did not blame God for any unfairness.

Again there was a time when God's angels gathered before the Lord and Satan was among them. And again God asked Satan where he came from.

"From going to and fro in the earth," answered Satan, "and from walking up and down in it."

"Have you considered My servant Job?" asked the Lord. "He is perfectly upright, and he fears God and avoids evil. He still keeps his good character even though you have done so much against him unfairly."

But Satan still would not agree that Job served God

because he sincerely loved God. Satan said, "A man will give anything for his life. If You would reach out and touch his body, he would curse You to Your face."

"You may do it," said the Lord. "His body is in your hands, but you must spare his life."

So Satan went forth from God's presence and smote Job with a terrible sickness. Job was covered with sore boils from the top of his head to the sole of his foot. In misery, he took a fragment of pottery and sat down among the ashes to scrape his sores.

Job's wife had had enough. She urged him, "Why don't you curse God? Then you would die. Why do you still trust in God's righteousness?"

Job answered his wife, "You speak like a foolish woman. When God brings something good into our lives, we receive it gladly. When He sees fit to bring trouble to us, should we not accept that as well?" In spite of all his troubles, Job still would not accuse God of being unfair in any way.

Job's Friends Come to Visit
Job 2:11–14:22

Eliphaz, Bildad, and Zophar were three of Job's friends. When they heard of the disasters that had come upon him, they agreed upon a time to visit Job to mourn with him and comfort him. The three men saw Job from a distance as they approached him. But Job's sickness and suffering made him look so different that they did not recognize him.

Job's three friends wept for Job in his suffering. They were so grieved that they tore their clothes and put dust upon their heads. Then they sat down in silence. For seven days they sat on the ground with their suffering friend and said nothing.

Finally Job spoke. "The day I was born is a cursed day. It is a day of darkness and death, not to be remembered or rejoiced in. Why did I not die when I was born? Then I could be in peace, but now I am tortured."

Eliphaz answered Job. "Will it grieve you if we talk to you? But how can we keep from speaking? You have instructed and helped many others, but now trouble has come upon you. Did you ever hear of anyone innocent or righteous being destroyed? It is those who sow wickedness that reap trouble. Seek the Lord, and do not despise His correction. Then you will be at peace and you will be blessed." Eliphaz seemed to think that there was some sin in Job's life and his troubles were punishment for it.

Job cried out, "Oh, that my grief could be weighed! It would be heavier than all the sand of the sea. I wish God would destroy me and I would die. I have done nothing against God. I am able to discern right and wrong."

Then Bildad asked Job, "Is God ever unfair? If you were pure and upright, surely God would prosper you. Consider all the fathers of the ages past. God does not cast away a perfect man."

Job said, "I know that is true, but who can be perfect before God? God is so great that He moves the mountains, shakes the earth, and controls the sun and the stars. He does great things that we cannot possibly understand or count. Even if I am righteous, He is so much more righteous that I could not speak with Him. If I tried to prove myself pure, my own words would condemn me.

"In this earth troubles come to the righteous and to the wicked. We cannot blame the Almighty or question what He does. There is no one to go between God and man to help us understand His ways. I wish I could understand why He causes me to suffer. Oh, that I could die!"

Then Zophar spoke to Job. "A multitude of words

will not justify you. You should be ashamed of your lies and mocking when you say you are clean and pure in the eyes of God. God should speak against you and show you His wisdom. Your punishment is less than you deserve. Can you understand God by searching? He is as high as heaven and deeper than hell, longer than the earth and broader than the sea. He knows everything about you. Put away your wickedness, and you will be lifted up and forget your misery."

Job felt deeply hurt by his friends' words. "No doubt you are the only ones who are wise, and when you die, wisdom will die with you!" he said. "I also have understanding as well as you. God has control of all things, and sometimes He causes the great to be destroyed. He overthrows the mighty and weakens the strong. I wish I could talk to God about these things. But you are making up lies and are not any help to me. It would be wise for you to hold your peace.

"Even if God slays me, I will trust in Him. I wish He would make me understand my sins instead of punishing me when I do not know why. I wish I were in the grave."

Discussion With Job

Job 15:1–31:40

Eliphaz again responded to Job's words. "You fill yourself with wind and say unprofitable things," he rebuked. "Are you the first man that was born? Do you know the secrets of God? What do you understand that we do not know? What is in your heart that you say such things before God? How can you say you are clean before Him? Behold, even the mighty heavens are not pure in comparison to Him."

"What miserable comforters you are!" declared Job. "I know all these things you are telling me. I could say the same to you if you were in my place. If you were suffering, I would say things to strengthen you and ease your grief. But nothing comforts me. God has delivered me to torture and weeping and scorn, but not for any wrong that I have done. If only I could plead with God!"

Bildad spoke again. "How long are you going to talk? Let us know when you are finished, and then we will speak. Why do you count us as vile beasts? A wicked man comes into darkness and snares. His own words bring him to destruction and terrors."

"How long will you vex me with your words?" cried Job. "It was not wickedness that brought all these things upon me. It is God that has taken away my glory and treated me like an enemy. I cry to Him, but He does not answer or give me justice. My relatives have failed me. My friends have forgotten me. My servants do not respond to me. Even my wife is a stranger. Have pity on me, O my friends!

"Oh, that my words were written in a book and graven in a rock. For I know that my Redeemer lives, and that He shall stand in the latter day upon the earth. And I know that after I am dead and my body is destroyed, yet in my flesh I shall see God."

Then Zophar replied, "Don't you know it has always been true that the wicked man's triumph is short? A hypocrite's joy is just for a moment. Though he be ever so great, he will be turned to destruction. He will not be at peace, and there will be no quietness for his spirit. Heaven and earth will finally expose his iniquity. God does this to wicked men."

Job answered, "Listen while I speak, and then you may mock on. Has my trouble been from man? If it were, there would be reason to have a troubled spirit. But take notice that my trouble is not from man, and put your hand over your mouth. I know the thoughts and the wickedness of which you accuse me. The things you say are false. How can you possibly comfort me?"

Still Job's visitors tried to convince him that there was sin in his life. But Job continued to insist that he was innocent. "Till I die I will not change my upright character," he declared. "I hold fast to righteousness.

My heart will not reproach me as long as I live."

Job began to talk of his past life, wishing that he could experience God's blessing as He had before. "Oh, that I were as in months past," he sighed. "Then God's light shone on my way and my children were about me. I was prosperous and everyone respected me. The aged rose to honor me, and princes and nobles held their peace in respect for my wisdom.

"The poor and the fatherless and the widows blessed me because I helped them. My reputation was well established. I expected many more good days.

"But now I am laughed at by people younger than I. Men of poor character make a joke of me. They abhor me and spit in my face. When I expected good, evil came upon me.

"Let God judge me. If I have walked in vanity or deceit, let all my labors be fruitless. If I have not been fair to my servants, how can I defend myself before God?—for He has made us all. If I have kept back food or clothing from the poor, let my arm fall from my shoulder blade and be broken. If I have put my trust in gold and my great wealth, or if I have worshiped false gods, I would deserve great punishment. If I have not used my land right, let thistles grow instead of wheat. My words are finished."

Lesson 4

Elihu Speaks and God Speaks

Job 32:1–40:5

A younger man named Elihu had been listening to the exchange between Job and his friends. Elihu was stirred up because Job kept justifying himself rather than glorifying God. He was also angered because Job's friends had condemned Job without being able to answer his questions. Finally Elihu burst out, "I kept silence because you are older, and because I thought older men should have more wisdom. But old men are not always wise, so I will also say what I think. I can no longer hold back my opinion.

"Listen, Job. You have said you are innocent, and God is treating you like an enemy. It is unjust to say such things about God. God is greater than man, and He does not need to give any reason for the things He does. God allows suffering and pain. God restores health like a youth's, and He delivers the soul of the man who confesses his sin.

"All these things God often does with men. You can be sure that the Almighty never deals unjustly. Is it proper to say to a king, 'You are wicked,' or to princes, 'You are ungodly'? How much more is it unfit to accuse Him who has made all the kings and princes? He will

never put upon man more than what is right.

"Surely it is good to say to God, 'I have been punished; I do not want to sin any more. If I have sinned, teach me what I do not realize, and I will sin no more.' It is not wise for you to insist that you are sinless. Should you say that you are more righteous than God? Does God gain anything from your righteousness? Does God lose anything if you are wicked? Wickedness or righteousness affects a man's life, but God's majesty is not changed by the things you do. Trust in God, for His judgments are fair.

"My heart trembles at the mighty greatness of God. He makes the small drops of water pour from the clouds. He spreads His clouds over the light. He directs the lightning, and the thunder is the roaring of His voice. He sends the snow on the earth, and His breath sends the frost and freezes the water. He sends the south wind to warm the earth again. He is perfect in knowledge! We cannot comprehend the things that He does. He is excellent in power and judgment."

And then God Himself spoke! Out of a whirlwind God said to Job, "Who is this that gives counsel without knowledge? Prepare yourself and answer Me. Where were you when I laid the foundations of the earth? Who laid out the measure for it and stretched the line for its building? On what is the earth's foundation fastened, and who laid the cornerstone?

"Who shut up the sea and told it how far it may come? Have you ever commanded the morning to come?

Have you searched the depth of the sea? Do you have power over the gates of death?

"Do you know how wide the earth is? Do you know where the light dwells and where the darkness is? Have you entered into the treasures of the snow or the treasures of the hail? Who makes it rain on the earth to satisfy the ground and make the buds and plants spring forth? Who are the parents of the rain, dew, ice, and frost?

"Can you bind Pleiades or loosen the bands of Orion? Can you bring forth Mazzaroth in his season or guide Arcturus and his sons? Do you know the laws of the heavens?

"Can you tell the clouds to send you water? Can you control the lightning and make it come and go at your pleasure? Can you provide food for the lions and ravens? Do you understand the ways of the wild goats? Who set the wild ass free to live in the wilderness away from the control of men? Can you make the wild ox work to gather in your harvest? Did you give the peacock his beautiful wings?

"Did you give the ostrich her feathers? She lays her eggs in the warm dust and leaves them, even though some foot may crush them or a wild beast may break them. God made her with that nature and without the wisdom to care for her young. But when she lifts up her foot, she can run much faster than a horse.

"Have you given the horse his strength? Can you make him afraid? He paws in the valley and runs to meet armed men in battle, unafraid of the spear.

"Is it by your wisdom that the hawk flies? Is it by your command that the eagle soars on high and builds her nest in the high places? She lives on the crags of the rocks and sees her prey far, far away. She goes where the slain are and brings blood for her young ones.

"Now, can he who argues with the Almighty instruct Him?" asked God. "Let him that criticizes God answer Me."

Job felt very, very small and unworthy when he thought of these things. He could not possibly give God instructions. "How wicked I am!" Job cried. "What shall I answer? I will put my hand over my mouth. I have spoken once, yes, twice, but I will speak no more."

Lesson 5

God Corrects and Blesses

Job 40:6–42:17

God spoke from the whirlwind again. "Prepare yourself and declare unto Me," He demanded of Job. "Will you speak against My judgment? Will you condemn Me to make yourself look righteous?

"Do you have an arm like God's? Can you thunder with a voice like His? Deck yourself with majesty and glory and beauty. Look around on all those who are proud and bring them low. Tread down the wicked and punish them. If you can do these things, then I will confess that your own hand can save you.

"Consider the behemoth that I made. He eats grass as an ox, and he has powerful strength. His bones are as strong as brass and iron. The mountains provide his food and the trees give him shade. The rivers give him water. He breaks through snares. Only the One who made him can control him.

"Consider the leviathan that I made. Can you catch him with a hook? Can you gentle him and use him for a servant? Can you make a pet of him? Or can you butcher him for a feast? Who can face his terrible teeth, or pierce his tight scales? No one is brave enough to stir him up to battle. Then who can stand against Me?

"To whom do I owe anything?" said the Lord. "Everything under heaven is Mine."

Job meekly answered, "I know that You can do everything, and no one can hide anything from You. 'Who is this that gives counsel without knowledge?' I have spoken things that I did not understand. Now I understand You better, and I abhor myself. I repent in dust and ashes."

Then the Lord spoke to Eliphaz. He said, "I am angry with you and your two friends. You have not spoken things that are right as Job has. Now you take seven bullocks and seven rams and go to my servant Job. Offer the animals for an offering for yourselves and let Job pray for you. His prayer will save you from the punishment you deserve, for you have not spoken things that are right as My servant Job has."

So Eliphaz, Bildad, and Zophar went and took animals for an offering. Job prayed for his friends.

Then God changed Job's life again and blessed him with twice as much as he had before. All Job's brothers and sisters and former friends came to see him. They ate at his house and mourned and comforted him over all the troubles he had borne. Everyone gave him money and gold.

Job became twice as rich as he had been before. He now had fourteen thousand sheep, six thousand camels, a thousand yoke of oxen, and a thousand she asses.

Job was also blessed with another family. He again had seven sons and three daughters, and his daughters were the most beautiful women in that land.

Job lived one hundred forty years after this. He was able to enjoy his blessings and to see his great-great grandsons. When Job died, he was an old man of many days.

The Book of Nature and Scripture
Psalm 19

1. The heavens high above
      Declare God's glory true;
    The firmament displays
      His handiwork anew.
    Day unto day declareth speech,
      And night to night doth knowledge teach.

2. Aloud they do not speak;
      They utter forth no word,
    Nor into language break;
      Their voice is never heard.
    Their line through all the earth extends,
      Their words to earth's remotest ends.

3. In them He for the sun
      Hath set a dwelling place;
    Rejoicing as a man
      Of strength, to run a race.
    He like a bridegroom in array,
      Comes from His chamber, bringing day.

4. His daily going forth
     Is from the end of heaven;
   The firmament to him
     Is for his circuit given.
   His circuit reaches to its ends,
     And everywhere his heat extends.

5. God's perfect law converts
     The soul in sin that lies;
   His testimony sure
     Doth make the simple wise;
   His statues just delight the heart;
     His holy precepts light impart.

6. The fear of God is clean,
     And ever doth endure;
   His judgments are all truth,
     And righteousness most pure.
   To be desired are they far more
     Than finest gold in richest store.

7. God's judgments to the taste
     More sweet than honey are,
   Than honey dropping from
     The comb, yes, sweeter far.
   In them Thy servant has a guard;
     In keeping them is great reward.

The All-Seeing God

Psalm 139

1.   Lord, Thou has searched me, and hast known
     My rising up and sitting down,
        And from afar Thy searching eye
        Beholds my thoughts that secret lie.

2.   The path I tread, my lying down,
     And all my ways—to Thee are known;
        For in my tongue no word can be,
        But, lo, O Lord, 'tis known to Thee.

3.   Behind, before me, Thou dost stand,
     And lay on me Thy mighty hand;
        Such knowledge is so high, so grand,
        'Tis more than I can understand.

4.   Oh, whither shall my footsteps fly,
     To flee Thy Spirit's searching eye?
        To what retreat shall I repair,
        And find not Thy great presence there?

5. If up to heaven I ascend,
   Thy presence surely will attend;
      If in the grave I find my place,
      Behold, again I meet Thy face!

6. If on the morning wings I flee
   And dwell in utmost parts of sea;
      There, too, Thy hand shall guide my way,
      And Thy right hand shall be my stay.

7. Or if I say, to shun Thine eye,
   In shades of darkness I will lie,
      Around me then the very night
      Will shine as does the noonday light.

8. I praise Thy skill when I survey
   The wonderful and fearful way
      That Thou has formed my earthly frame.
      'Twas from Thy hand, my God, I came.

9. How precious are Thy thoughts of me,
   In number more than sand of sea!
      How faithful is Thy constant care,
      When I awake Thou still art there.

10. The wicked Thou wilt slay, O God;
    Depart from me, ye men of blood;
       I grieve to hear their words profane,
       Who take Thy holy Name in vain.

The Good Shepherd

Psalm 23

1. The Lord my shepherd feeds me,
    And I no want shall know;
    In pastures green He leads me,
    By streams which gently flow.

2. He doth, when ill betides me,
    Restore me from distress;
    For His Name's sake He guides me
    In paths of righteousness.

3. Thy rod and staff shall cheer me
    When passing death's dark vale;
    Thou, Lord, wilt still be near me,
    And I shall fear no ill.

4. My food Thou dost appoint me,
    Prepared before my foes;
    With oil Thou dost anoint me;
    My cup of bliss o'erflows.

5. Thy goodness shall not leave me,
   Thy mercy still shall guide,
   Until God's house receive me,
   Forever to abide.

The Works of God

Psalm 104:1–24

1.   O bless the Lord, my soul. O God,
    Adorned with glorious rays
Of honor, light, and majesty,
    To Thee be greatest praise.

2.   He lays His beams in waters deep;
    He spreads His curtain sky;
He rides on chariot clouds, and walks
    On wings of wind that fly.

3.   He laid foundations for the earth,
    And clothed it with the seas.
He bound the ocean in its place,
    And sent cool springs to please.

4.   The donkeys wild, and beasts of fields
    Come to the springs to drink.
The fowls of heaven sing God's praise
    In trees along their brink.

5. The hills are watered by the streams;
    The earth is satisfied;
And grass comes forth for cattle's need.
    With herbs man is supplied.

6. The stately cedars full of sap—
    On Lebanon that stand,
Where birds find shelter for their nests—
    Were planted by God's hand.

7. Wild goats a place of refuge find
    Upon the mountains high;
The conies also to the rocks
    Do for their safety fly.

8. God sets the moon on high to mark
    The seasons as they go;
He makes the sun at proper time
    Its going down to know.

9. He brings the darkness, when the beasts
    Of forest creep abroad.
The lions roar in quest of prey,
    And seek their meat from God.

10. With rising sun they all return,
    And lie down in their dens;
Man goes to work and labors there
    Till evening comes again.

11. How manifold Thy works, O Lord!
   In wisdom they are made.
   In all the earth so great and wide
   Thy riches are displayed.

God's Goodness

Psalm 107

1. Oh, that all men would praise the Lord!
    His goodness and His works record.
    > The longing soul He satisfies
    > And fills the hungry soul that cries.

2. Sad rebels bound with iron chains
    Cried to the Lord in dark and pains;
    > He saved them from distress and fright;
    > He broke their bands and gave them light.

3. Oh, that all men would praise the Lord!
    His goodness and His works record;
    > He cut the iron bars in two,
    > And all the gates of brass broke through.

4. Afflicted fools because of sin
    Draw near to death all sick within,
    > But when they cry to God He hears
    > And heals and saves them from their fears.

5. Oh, that all men would praise the Lord!
   His goodness and His works record,
   Give thanks and offer sacrifice;
   Rejoice in works beyond all price.

6. All those in ships on waters deep
   Behold God's works as great waves leap
   And toss their ship while storms do blow.
   As drunk, they stagger to and fro.

7. They cry to God in their distress
   And soon the raging storm is less.
   He stills the waves and calms the sea
   And brings them where they want to be.

8. Oh, that all men would praise the Lord!
   His goodness and His works record,
   Exalt Him in assembled crowd,
   Give praise and sing and shout aloud!

God's Word

Psalm 119

1. Blest are the undefiled in heart,
   Whose ways are right and clean;
   Who never from Thy Law depart,
   But on Thy precepts lean.

2. Blest are the men who keep Thy Word,
   And practice Thy commands;
   With their whole heart they seek the Lord,
   And serve Him with their hands.

3. How shall the young man cleanse his way
   And guard his life from sin?
   By taking heed to what You say
   To hide Thy Word within.

4. With my whole heart I've sought Thy face;
   Oh, let me never stray
   From Thy commands, O God of grace,
   Nor tread the sinner's way.

5. Thy Word I've hid within my heart
    That it may stay with me
To warn me when my steps would start
    To sin and turn from Thee.

6. To meditate Thy precepts, Lord,
    Shall be my sweet employ;
My soul shall not forget Thy Word;
    Thy Word is all my joy.

7. Deal kindly with Thy servant, Lord,
    That I may live to Thee;
Open mine eyes to read Thy Word,
    And wondrous things to see.

8. Oh, that the Lord would guide my ways
    To keep His statutes still!
Oh, that my God would grant me grace
    To know and do His will!

9. Make me to walk in Thy commands,
    This path is my delight.
Incline my heart, my head, my hands
    To cleave unto the right.

10. Oh, how I love Thy holy Law!
    Through all the day I find
My meditations there can draw
    Sweet rest and peace of mind.

11. 'Tis like the sun, a heavenly light,
        That guides us all the day;
     And through the dangers of the night,
        A lamp to lead our way.

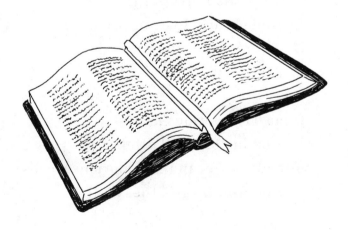

Praise

Psalm 145

1. I will extol Thee, O my God,
    And praise Thee, O my King;
   Yea, every day and evermore
    Thy praises I will sing.

   Refrain
   Every day will I bless Thee;
   Every day will I bless Thee;
   And I will praise, will praise Thy Name
   Forever and ever.

2. Great is the Lord, our mighty God,
    And greatly to be praised;
   His greatness is unsearchable,
    Above all glory raised.

3. Upon Thy glorious majesty
    And honor I will dwell,
   And all Thy grand and glorious works
    And all Thy greatness tell.

4. The Lord our God is good to all,
From Him all blessing flows;
On all His works His tender love
And mercy He bestows.

Psalm 100

1. Ye nations round the earth, rejoice
Before the Lord, your sovereign King;
Serve Him with cheerful heart and voice,
With all your tongues His glory sing.

2. The Lord is God; 'tis He alone
Doth life, and breath, and being give:
We are His work, and not our own,
The sheep that on His pastures live.

3. Enter His gates with songs of joy,
With praises to His courts repair,
And make it your divine employ
To pay your thanks and honors there.

4. The Lord is good, the Lord is kind;
Great is His grace, His mercy sure;
And the whole race of man shall find
His truth from age to age endure.

A Prayer in Danger

Psalm 57

1. Be merciful to me, O Lord
       Until these woes be overpast;
    Beneath Thy wings that care afford
       There's refuge safe through all the blast.

2. To God supreme I make my cry;
       He brings to pass all things for me.
    He sends His help from heaven high,
       And saves from dangers speedily.

3. As lions fierce that seek their prey,
       With teeth as spears, and fire of hate,
    My foes pursue my lonely way;
       I lie to sleep at danger's gate.

4. Be Thou exalted, God most high,
       Above the heavens be Thy praise;
    Above the earth we glorify
       Thy Name for all Thy wondrous ways.

5. The net prepared to catch my feet,
   The pit they dug to bring my fall,
   In both of them my foes will meet
   The doom they planned for my downfall.

6. My heart is fixed, O God, on Thee;
   My heart and voice a song shall raise,
   And all the pow'rs that in me be
   Shall rise up early and give praise.

7. Among the people I will show
   Thy mercy great unto the skies,
   And cause the nations all to know
   Thy truths above the heavens rise.

8. Be Thou exalted, God most high,
   Above the heavens be Thy praise;
   Above the earth we glorify
   Thy Name for all Thy wondrous ways.

Pleading for Pardon

Psalm 51

1. In Thy great lovingkindness, Lord
    Be merciful to me;
   In Thy compassions great, blot out
    All my iniquity.

2. Oh, wash iniquity away
    Cleanse me from guilt within:
   For my transgressions I confess;
    I ever see my sin.

3. Against Thee only have I sinned,
    Done evil in Thy sight,
   That when Thou speakest Thou art just,
    And in Thy judging, right.

4. Behold, in sinful form I came
    Into this life at birth,
   But Thou desirest truth within
    And wisdom of great worth.

5. With hyssop sprinkle me to purge
   And wash my soul from sin;
   Then whiter than the snow I'll be,
   All pure and clean within.

6. All my iniquities blot out,
   And hide them from Thy view,
   Create a clean heart, Lord, in me
   A spirit right renew.

7. And from Thy gracious presence, Lord,
   Oh, cast me not away;
   The Holy Spirit do not take
   Away from me, I pray.

8. The joy of Thy salvation, Lord,
   To me again restore;
   And with Thy Spirit free, do Thou
   Uphold me evermore.

9. Then I will teach transgressors, too,
   In Thy most holy ways,
   And sinners will be turned to Thee
   To sing aloud Thy praise.

10. My tongue shall sing aloud of Thee
    And give the sacrifice:
    A broken and a contrite heart
    Lord, Thou wilt not despise.

The Righteous and the Wicked

Psalm 1

1. How blest the man that does not stray
        Where wicked counsel tempts his feet;
    Who stands not in the sinners' way,
        And sits not in the scorner's seat.
    But in God's law he takes delight,
    And meditates both day and night.

2. He shall be like the tree that springs
        Where streams of water gently glide;
    Which plenteous fruit in season brings,
        And ever green its leaves abide.
    Thus shall prosperity attend
    The good man's work, till life shall end.

3. Not so ungodly men, for they
        Like chaff before the wind are driven;
    Hence they'll not stand in judgment day,
        Nor mingle with the saints in heaven.
    The Lord approves the good man's path,
    But sinners' ways shall end in wrath.

What a Day May Bring Forth

Boast not thyself of to morrow; for thou knowest not what a day may bring forth. (Proverbs 27:1)

"Are we going to the sale in Grantland tomorrow?" asked Morris on Friday evening.

"Would you like to?" questioned Father.

"Oh, yes!" chorused Stanley and Owen.

"I hope we get a doll house. Could we, Father?" begged Alice.

Father smiled at Alice. "Better not count on it. They might not be selling a doll house. You never know what you will find at such a community sale. I was thinking of going to the sale, though. My work is well caught up in the shop, and I really have nothing else planned for tomorrow. I think I'll take that set of truck wheels along. I may be able to get something for them, and they are just cluttering the ground out behind the shop."

Saturday dawned a lovely summer day. Morris hurried with his chores, eager for the main event of the day. Right at the end of the morning routine, Morris glanced out the window and exclaimed, "Here comes somebody!" A young woman was walking in the drive, looking about uncertainly.

Mother answered the timid knock at the door. "I'm sorry to bother you," faltered the lady, "but I'm having car trouble and I wonder if I could use your telephone."

"Certainly," answered Mother kindly. "Come in; the telephone is right here. Do you need the directory?"

The visitor dialed a number and waited anxiously. "He must not be home," she murmured. "Maybe I'll try Dean's." But there was no response there either. "I don't know what to do," she said. "I don't get any answer, and I don't know who else to ask for help."

"Where is your car?" asked Mother. "My husband is a mechanic, so maybe he can help you. Peter, run and find Father. He might be out behind the shop getting the wheels he wants to sell."

Father came in and asked a few questions about the nature of the problem. The boys helped him tow the car in and spent the next hour watching the repair process.

"Thank you so much!" gushed Miss Himmon when Father had finished his work. "I don't know what I would have done without you folks. And thank you for the chat and the papers." She waved to Mother, who had given her a few tracts.

"Now let's load those wheels," Father suggested. The boys ran and wheeled them to the car as Father opened the trunk. "Where is the other one?" asked Father. "There are four."

The boys dashed back to the lot behind the shop, and Father followed them. They searched the tall grass. They sorted the heap of metal scraps and parts.

They scanned the yard and garden. They stood and pondered. "Do you know anything about the fourth wheel?" Father asked Mother.

"No, I don't. But I have another interruption to suggest. Aunt Miriam just called. Uncle Franks have been to Ketter's Orchard and found a surplus of ripe cherries. They are selling them very cheaply to get rid of them before they spoil. Uncle Franks brought a truckload and offered us some. Do we want them? They will have to be canned today."

"That sounds like a good chance," reasoned Father. "We can't seem to find our sale items anyway." So a trip was made to Uncle Franks for cherries. The whole family joined in the project of canning the fruit.

As Morris seeded cherries, he kept one eye on the clock. Could they still attend part of the sale? By midafternoon he was dismissed from the job while Mother and the girls finished the canning and cleaning up.

Morris hurried to the lot behind the shop for one more look around. "Where is that wheel? Why, here it is! Hidden in a patch of tall grass and weeds. I'm sure we looked through here this morning." He lifted the wheel to roll it around the shop. "Ouch! That was a bee! Ouch! A whole nest of them!" Morris dropped the wheel and fled from the insects that suddenly swarmed around him.

"Mother, I think—I got—a hundred bee stings!" he panted as he sank onto a kitchen chair. "I feel sort of funny, like I can't breathe," he added.

"I think we had better get him to the doctor," observed Father. "Can you handle the cherries, Sheila and Lorene?"

"The last ones are boiling. Turn them off in ten minutes," instructed Mother.

As quickly as possible, Morris was taken to the doctor's office. The doctor gave him a shot which made him feel better right away. He also gave them some medicine in case this happened again.

On the way home, Morris lamented, "We had only one thing planned for today, and we didn't even get that done."

Father chuckled. "We didn't get to the sale, did we? But I am satisfied that God had this day planned according to His will."

Slow to Anger

He that is slow to anger is better than the mighty; and he that ruleth his spirit than he that taketh a city. (Proverbs 16:32)

"Just think, our own horses!" exclaimed Sanford.

"But it's up to us to make them good horses," said Ray. The brothers hung on the corral fence watching the yearling colts.

Father had just told them he would give them each a colt. He would help to break and train them, and then the horses would belong to the boys. Ray and Sanford were both good riders and galloped Father's horses all over the cattle ranch. But to have horses all their own . . . ! The boys thrilled with eagerness.

"I like Ebony," Ray said. "He's going to be a powerful horse someday. And it will take some power to break him. He's got a strong spirit."

"I'm afraid I wouldn't be strong enough to handle one like that," confessed Sanford, who was a few years younger. "I think Sandy is beautiful." He was watching the small filly with a white blaze on her face.

Since the colts were already halter broken, the boys began their training by leading the horses on short ropes. "Giddap!" they called as they started the colts walking, and "Whoa!" as they stopped and held them.

"Giddap" and "Whoa," they said, again and again, until the colts responded to the words before the boys gave a physical signal.

By and by they changed to a long rope. This gave the animal more freedom so that it could walk in a large circle around the trainer, following spoken commands. But Ebony seemed confused when Ray backed off and called, "Giddap!" He started toward the boy, who backed off farther and shouted, "Whoa!" Several times Ray tried, but Ebony always came to him instead of staying the rope's length away and going in a circle. Finally the frustrated boy grabbed a light branch from a nearby tree and switched Ebony in the face. The colt kept his distance then. He nervously made a large circle, but he no longer heeded the commands as well as usual.

After the workout that day, Sanford sighed. "I don't know if I'll ever learn to manage Sandy on the long rope. I always have to go back and hold the rope near to her. She did seem to get the idea of going around me, though."

"I had a little trouble with that, too," said Ray. "But I got it across. I just had to show Ebony that I mean what I say."

The next day Ray had to chase Ebony around the corral several times before he could get his hand on the halter. He felt impatience rising within him, but kept control of himself. "He's probably afraid because I beat him yesterday," Ray realized. "Here, Ebony, let's get your bridle on."

But Ebony was not cooperating that day. He lifted his head when Ray brought the bridle near. He turned his head to one side and then pulled to the other. Ray's patience was wearing thin. He pulled roughly on the halter and jerked the colt's head around. "You know what I want," he growled. "This isn't anything new."

Sanford already had his colt bridled and was putting her through a review of the familiar commands. He had to start all over with the long rope because Sandy didn't seem to remember anything about it. But it was easier that day. He got Sandy to circle him, and then he gradually let out more rope. "Good girl, Sandy," praised Sanford, rubbing the colt's neck after the exercise. "You're learning after all. I'll get you a carrot for a reward."

"Never beat your horses," Father had taught the boys. "That spoils the trust you want them to have in you." But there were times when Ray came to the very end of his patience. His temper snapped and it seemed that he could not help beating his horse. It became harder to catch Ebony. Ray often had to use a piece of carrot or some other treat to coax Ebony to him.

The difference between the two animals grew greater all the time. "How did you make out with the saddle?" asked Ray the day they first put them on the colts.

"Sandy was wonderful!" exclaimed Sanford. "I think she was curious. She kept sticking her nose around to see what I was doing when I fastened the girth. But she was quiet about it."

246

"Sandy likes you," commented Ray. "She'd let you do anything to her."

"I never do anything to hurt her," answered Sanford.

"I had to get a little rough with Ebony," admitted Ray. "He didn't know what to make of the saddle either, but I got it on and he found out that it didn't hurt him."

The day came when the boys dared to mount the saddle. Now they could begin teaching their horses to respond to signals from the hands and knees of the rider. The next step would be to use only the hand and knee signals and no longer give spoken commands. There was much training to do yet, but sitting in the saddle at last seemed like a great milestone. It was especially satisfying for Sanford. When he dismounted, he patted and praised Sandy with special affection.

Ebony was nervous about the affair. Ray was nervous, too, but he was determined. He managed to hold his seat while Ebony pranced around. The colt kicked a few times and danced sideways, not knowing what might happen with the boy on his back. Ray talked softly to the colt, and Ebony finally calmed down. The boy apparently wasn't on his back to beat him.

The brothers hung on the corral fence after this ride. Sandy trotted up to the fence and nuzzled Sanford. Ebony had escaped as soon as he was released. He seemed to prefer avoiding his master as much as he could.

Ray gazed across the corral. "I wish . . ." His

words trailed off.

Sanford turned his attention from his horse to his brother. "What do you wish?"

"Sanford, you're having much better success than I am," Ray finally confessed. "I thought I was conquering my horse with power. But he isn't conquered. I have spoiled so much by my anger."

The Firstfruits

Honour the Lord with thy substance, and with the firstfruits of all thine increase:

So shall thy barns be filled with plenty, and thy presses shall burst out with new wine. (Proverbs 3:9,10)

1 Gwen Furlam snipped the thread and gave a little "hurrah." The second rug was finished—and it was superior to the first. The greens, grays, and browns blended in a pleasing pattern as the long braid wound around and around in an oval shape.

2 Many hours had gone into the making of this rug. First she had cut strips of material from old clothes Mother had stored in the attic for such projects. Then came the pleasant task of braiding the strips. With a little practice it wasn't hard to make an even braid. The most challenging part was getting the braid stitched together in a nice oval that would lie flat.

3 Gwen hoped to earn a little money by selling braided rugs. She would soon be at the end of the supply in the attic, but with a little income she could get plenty of sturdy used clothes at the secondhand shop.

4 Gwen's dreaming was interrupted by a knock at the door. Mrs. Barwick had come for her usual purchase of farm eggs, and Gwen brought them from the cooler for her.

5 "What a lovely rug!" exclaimed Mrs. Barwick, noticing that it was newly made. "Did you make it?"

6 "Yes, I just finished it a minute before you knocked."

7 "You will probably treasure that to use in your own house someday," suggested Mrs. Barwick.

8 "Well," responded Gwen, "I really was thinking of selling it."

9 "Selling it! What's your price?"

10 "Mother said I might ask twelve dollars."

11 "I'll take it along right now if I may." Mrs. Barwick had her purse open again and pulled out a ten-dollar bill and two ones. "As soon as I saw that rug, I knew that's exactly what I would like to give my niece for a wedding present. You don't know how this pleases me."

12 "It pleases me to make the sale," responded Gwen. "You might want to press the rug if you don't give it right away. We lay a new rug under a mattress for a few days. That makes it lie nice and flat."

13 "Thank you, I'll do that."

14 After Mrs. Barwick left, Gwen fingered the three bills as though she needed to make sure they were real.

15 "My first rug money," she marveled. "Of course, part of it is Father and Mother's, and part of it I'll put in the offering at church. I'll want a little for rug materials, and I'll probably put some into savings."

16 But the next time she went to church, Gwen changed her plans. The minister announced that there had been a fire at Piney Run Children's Home. Most of the living

quarters had been destroyed, and they would appreciate any help in the cost and work of rebuilding. The minister also encouraged his people to give clothing or other household items to help replace what was lost.

17 "My first rug!" thought Gwen. "It's not as nice as the one I sold, but maybe they would be glad for it. And I wonder if Father and Mother would let me give all of the twelve dollars for the building fund."

18 Gwen's parents approved her plans, and the money and rug were given. Gwen was not sorry, but as she began the next rug she realized how near the end of her business she could be. The remaining materials would only make a small rug. If she did not sell that one, she would have no means of getting more material.

19 But Gwen's rug making was put aside when Mother promised Gwen's help to Mrs. Franklin, who wanted a helper for some housecleaning. For several afternoons one week they scrubbed and dusted until every room sparkled. Then finally they tackled the attic.

20 Mrs. Franklin pointed to a stack of boxes in one corner. "There is something I'd like to get rid of," she said. "When I worked in a sewing factory, I used to collect the rolls of wide binding that were discarded whenever we finished the lot of garments that the binding was used on. I thought they could be used for a craft project sometime, but I never did anything with them and I'm not likely to begin at this age. Do you have any ideas?"

Gwen opened a box and caught her breath at the

vision of rugs that bloomed before her eyes. "I'd love to use something like this for braided rugs!" she exclaimed. "Could I buy them?"

"Buy them!" Mrs. Franklin laughed. "I got them for nothing, and I'd be glad to have you take them out of my way."

"Oh, Mother, just think!" exclaimed Gwen that evening. "Here I thought I might not be able to make any more rugs. Now I have a whole mountain of strips all ready cut, perfectly straight, and in all colors!"

"I believe the Lord is blessing you for honoring Him with the beginning of your work," replied Mother with a warm smile.

Flattery's Net

A man that flattereth his neighbour spreadeth a net for his feet. (Proverbs 29:5)

Neil Grayson helped carry some of the smaller boxes from the truck into his new home. His little sisters tagged along, hugging their rag dolls and asking questions. "What's in that box? Where are you going to keep your bird nests? Do you like these winding stairs?"

Neil's bicycle came off the truck. "Where will you put that?" wondered Annie. "We don't have a garage here. Where will you keep your rabbits?"

"There's a little shed behind the house. Maybe my bicycle can go in there," answered Neil.

"And the rabbits, too?" suggested Debbie.

"I don't think so. It doesn't have windows and the rabbits would want light and air." Neil walked over to the wire cage sitting on the ground under the tree. "You're crowded in there, I know," he told his pets. "Be patient. Father said he could buy some pens to set beside the shed."

As Neil pushed his bicycle toward the shed, he saw a boy about his own size at the fence of the next property. The boy smiled and waved to him. Neil waved back. Would this be a good neighbor? Neil hoped so.

The shed was not empty. In one corner stood a cardboard box full of tin cans and other junk. There was a pile of thin boards along one wall and a roll of chicken wire beside it. Neil looked around the rest of the shed and then back to the boards and wire. An idea began to grow. Rabbit pens! Neil went to find father.

A few days later the family "across the fence" came to visit the Graysons. Neil took Harold out to show him the rabbit cages he was building. "We found these old boards in the little shed," he explained. "Father thought he would have to buy pens for my rabbits, but I think I can make some with these."

Harold looked at the thin boards and thought, "How flimsy! But I want my new neighbor to feel accepted, so I'll have to say something nice."

"You're doing a good job," Harold complimented. "You're a good builder. I wish I could make something that nice."

The rabbits were still crowded in the wire cage in which they had made the moving trip. They looked matted and sickly. Was that from traveling and being crowded? Or were they not being fed properly? Again Harold decided to say something that would make the other boy feel good. "What nice rabbits!" he exclaimed.

Neil's face beamed. "I was a little bit worried about them," he confessed. "They seem a bit listless. I wondered if I should have a veterinarian see them.

"Oh, they'll be all right," Harold said soothingly. "They probably miss their old, familiar home. They look pretty good to me. When you get them into your grand new pens, they'll hop around as lively as can be.

"I think you'll have a really good business with your rabbits," Harold continued. "I can see you are good at taking care of them, and you do a beautiful job of building cages. If you want to sell rabbits, I think there would be a good market for them at the farmer's auction every week."

The next day Neil worked again on his rabbit cages. "Rather wobbly," he observed. "But Harold seemed to think they were pretty good. Maybe they'll serve better than they look. I could use some more of these thin boards to make them stronger, but I think I'll save them to build more pens. I would like to have a whole row if this is going to be a profitable business."

Neil gently put the rabbits into their new cages. He gave them some pellets and pulled a handful of grass for each one. Then he bade his pets "good night" and gathered up the tools and scraps from his building project.

In the morning Neil hurried out to see if his rabbits had perked up. He rounded the corner of the house and stopped abruptly. The cages were a wreck! The fragile boards were splintered, and wire netting hung down crazily from one corner.

"My rabbits!" Neil cried, and ran toward one furry heap at the corner of the shed. Bronco was dead, no doubt about that. Samantha was too, and there was Hazy, torn and partly eaten by some animal. What had happened? Where were Liskin and Hobo? Neil wanted to cry.

Father walked across the yard and stood beside Neil, viewing the disaster. "Looks like dogs' work," he said kindly, laying his hand on Neil's shoulder.

"I just finished the cages and put the rabbits in them last night," lamented Neil.

Father picked up a broken board and broke it again in his hands. "I'm sorry I didn't take time to direct your building better. Did you expect these cages to be secure?"

"I knew they were awfully flimsy. But Harold said they were so good; I guess I let his praise override my common sense."

"If you hadn't been flattered by his words, you might still have your rabbits," commented Father.

Disappointed Brothers

He also that is slothful in his work is brother to him that is
a great waster. (Proverbs 18:9)

"Put your book down, Ernest, and get something
done on your carving," scolded Clarence. "You haven't
touched that dog for a week, have you?"

"Oh, don't worry," Ernest answered his brother. "I'll
get at it one of these days." He strolled over to the table
and stroked his piece of carving. "Now I've touched it.
It's no use trying when I don't feel like it. It just doesn't
go right when I'm not interested." Ernest curled up
with his book again.

Wood carving was more than a hobby for these
Swiss boys. The bit of income that their carvings earned
was a welcome help in providing the family's needs.

Clarence whittled rapidly for a few minutes and
then held up his block of wood. He squinted his eyes
and cocked his head, trying to see in his mind the
finished figure. "Won't do," he murmured, tossing the
block into the box of kindling by the stove.

Taking a new block, he scratched a few lines on it
with his sharp knife. The sketch of a squirrel appeared
under his hands. But he had placed it back too far on
the block. There would not be room for the tail unless it

was tight against the body. Clarence wanted to carve the tail in a waving position. He liked his animal figures to look as if they were in action. Into the stove went the squirrel block, marked only with the sketch lines.

Clarence picked up another carving block and went to work on a new squirrel. This one he planned more carefully, and soon he was carving away large chips to produce the rough shape of the animal. Then he picked up his mallet and a fine chisel. Carefully he shaped the smaller details around the squirrel's head and paws.

A few days later something inspired Ernest again and he picked up his carving tools. He was putting the finishing touches on his dog when Clarence joined him. "I think I'll make a chalet today," decided Clarence, choosing a square piece from the pile of pine blocks. He quickly carved a few sketch lines to show the shape of his little house, and then he proceeded to whittle away the top corners.

Ernest set his finished dog on the shelf with their other completed carvings. "What shall I try next?" He picked up a carving booklet and looked at several designs in it.

"Oh, now I trimmed off the part I need for a chimney," grumbled Clarence. He tossed his carving into the kindling box and looked over the blocks for another square piece.

"You could still use that one if you made it a little smaller," suggested Ernest. "You waste such a great deal of wood."

258

"I'd rather start with a fresh piece than to whittle around trying to fix something. I don't like to change plans after I have something started."

"But you'd get more done if you stuck to your pieces and finished them."

"You're a good one to talk," laughed Clarence. "I'll easily have more pieces than you. If you wouldn't be so lazy, you'd get a lot more done, too."

Ernest soon flipped the booklet shut and dropped it on the table. "I don't think I'll start anything else today."

When Uncle Conrad and his son arrived a week later, the boys each had seven wooden carvings on the shelf. They would ski together down the mountain to Lucerne. Mr. Karl had a wood carving shop there, and he sold carvings for many boys of the Swiss Alps.

Cousin Peter pulled the pack off his back and opened it to show his collection of carvings. His cousins gasped in astonishment. Peter had done as much as the two brothers together!

"What a beautiful horse!" exclaimed Clarence.

"I like your bear cubs," Ernest said in admiration. Some of Peter's work was indeed excellent. Others of his pieces were average, and some were not quite as good as his cousins' work.

"I want to get a pair of skis with the money I get for these," Peter told his cousins. "Marcus should have bigger skis. If I get my own, he can have the ones I'm using."

"We need new boots," said Ernest and Clarence.

Uncle Conrad and Peter stayed for the night. In the morning the boys all packed up their carvings to carry on their backs. Clarence and Ernest were a bit embarrassed at the skimpy size of their packs compared to Peter's. But they put uncomfortable feelings aside as they set off down the snowy slopes with Uncle Conrad. It was a lovely morning to be out in the winter beauty. Below them Lake Lucerne sparkled in the sunshine.

Clarence earned twelve francs for his seven carvings, and Ernest received thirteen.

In the shoe shop the brothers admired the heavy padded ski boots. They really didn't expect to get something that special. But they were dismayed to find that they could not even pay for the common boots such as they wore. Their money together would not buy one pair the size they needed. Twenty-nine francs was the price marked.

"What shall we do?" whispered Ernest.

Clarence studied the cracks in the toes of his boots. "I guess the only thing to do is go back home and work at carving as if we mean business."

"I know I'm going to try harder to get more done," determined Ernest.

Joined Hands

Though hand join in hand, the wicked shall not be unpunished: but the seed of the righteous shall be delivered. (Proverbs 11:21)

Clara tore her eyes away from the window and picked up her pencil again. "I must quit dreaming and get this English done," she told herself. But it was so beautiful outside with the snow dancing and swirling in the air. It would surely improve their sledding track, which had worn bare in some spots.

"Oh, but there will be no sledding," Clara reminded herself. Neighbor Mullen had complained about damage to his winter crop in the field on which they had been sledding. Just that morning Brother Eby had announced that their recess limits would again be within the playground fence.

It stopped snowing by noon, but several inches had accumulated. The children were eager to enjoy the smooth new playground. As they packed up their lunch things, a loud knock sounded at the door.

Brother Eby opened the door and was greeted by a tall stranger. "Hello, I'm Brad Forrest, and this is my wife, Twila. We'd like to visit your school if we may."

"You are welcome to visit," invited Brother Eby.

"We are just finishing lunch and will dismiss for recess now."

Mr. Forrest explained their interest in starting a Christian school. They were visiting friends in the community, who recommended that they come and see Eagle Creek School.

"I will be glad to talk with you," said Brother Eby. He turned to the waiting children. "Barbara and Clara may design a track for snowtag. Anyone who would rather build snowmen may do so at the far end of the playground. And stay inside the fence," he reminded. Then he dismissed the rows one at a time.

Barbara and Clara each set out on a curve across the playground to mark a large circle. Behind each one marched a few other children, tramping down the snow for a good path.

The older boys started rolling up a few balls for a huge snowman. Leon paused to lean on the fence and to scan the smooth slope below. A plot of snow-decked pines shared the hill with Mr. Mullen's field. Below the slope, a country road curved across the landscape and disappeared behind the trees.

Titus joined Leon at the fence—and just then a pickup rounded a bend at the edge of the pines and slid into the ditch. The driver jumped out and looked at the snowbanks that held his truck.

"What's up?" asked Raymond, joining the two on the fence. Soon half a dozen boys hung on the fence, studying the situation below. "If we were sledding, we could be down there to help push him out," commented Joe.

"Couldn't we go and help him anyway?" suggested Leon.

"Brother Eby said we must stay inside the fence," reminded Brendon.

"He meant we should stay off the field," Joe corrected. "He wouldn't be against helping someone who is stuck."

"We could go down through the pines and not touch the field," Titus pointed out.

"Shouldn't we ask first?" wondered Andrew.

"He's busy with the Forrests, and we ought to hurry if we're going." So saying, Joe trotted to the corner of the playground. He sprang over the fence, entered the woods, and turned down the hill. Four or five others followed.

Andrew and Brendon paused on the fence. Andrew looked toward the school. "I don't feel right without asking."

"Where's everybody going?" shouted John when he noticed the exodus.

"Somebody is stuck down there," answered Brendon. "We're going to help push them out."

"Let's go, too!" Another stream of children hopped over the fence. Andrew and Brendon went along.

The snowtag trampers stopped in their tracks and stared. Soon they were at the fence. "What are they doing?" asked Clara.

"I don't know," Loretta answered.

"Let's go see," suggested Lena Jane.

"We're not allowed to go over the fence," protested Dorothy.

"They did."

"If everybody else does, we won't get into trouble for it," Mabel reasoned.

More children climbed the fence and disappeared into the pines. Clara paused and looked back. "Aren't you coming, Dorothy?"

"I don't think we should."

"But if everybody else goes, I don't want to be left out. You make me feel like I'm being bad," complained Clara.

"I'd feel like I was being bad if I went, too," answered Dorothy.

Clara hesitated. But then she turned and declared, "I'm going with everybody else."

Only Dorothy was left with a handful of the youngest children. She realized that they would probably go along, too, if she did. "But no, I just wouldn't feel right," she thought. To the children she said, "Come on, let's make a snowman."

"This is the longest recess we ever had," declared Eric.

"It does seem long," agreed Dorothy. "Maybe Brother Eby is giving us extra time so that he can talk with the visitors."

Finally someone appeared at the fence. It was a

264

group of girls helping Clara to walk. "Oh, Dorothy, I wish I had listened to you," moaned Clara. "I slipped on a log and hurt my ankle."

The group was nearly at the schoolhouse door when the boys came swarming over the fence. "Just in time," gasped Eugene, looking at his watch. A minute later the bell rang and everybody hurried into the school. They wanted to tell the teacher about their adventure, but their disobedience made them hesitate.

However, poor Clara could not hide her problem. "Brother Eby, I must have sprained my ankle," she blurted with tears in her eyes.

"What happened?" he asked.

"I—I slipped on a log in the snow."

"You slipped on a log? Where?" The teacher was puzzled.

"In the woods."

"In the woods? Lena Jane, go to the supply closet," he directed. "I think there is an elastic bandage on the shelf with the first aid kit. Bring it here, and then you may help Clara wrap her ankle tightly.

"Now, how did you come to be in the woods?" Brother Eby turned to Clara again.

"I—I wanted to see what everybody else was doing," she sobbed.

The rest of the children were all in their seats by this time. Brother Eby turned and looked over their sober faces. "Who else was in the woods?" he asked.

All over the room hands went up to identify the

guilty ones. Brother Eby placed an extra chair beside Clara's desk and instructed her to rest her bandaged ankle on it. Then he walked to the front of the room. "I have a special assignment for you," he said. "Everyone who was outside the fence this recess shall write a paragraph explaining why he was. I want those who were not outside the fence to write what they did at recess. Have your papers finished before the next dismissal."

Mr. and Mrs. Forrest were quietly observing from chairs at the back of the room. Brother Eby gave them a copy of his schedule for the afternoon classes. Then he called the first grade class. "We will do a page in your phonics book, and then Dorothy may help you write your sentences about recess," he told the children.

The next day the children received the punishment for their disobedience. "Brother Nathan Carder has offered to lead us on a hike through the woods to observe animal tracks and see the geese that winter on his pond," announced Brother Eby. "I have decided that those who were in the woods yesterday will lose that privilege today. The ones who obeyed yesterday will go with Brother Nathan, and the rest of us will stay here and have our regular classes."

Grievous Words

A soft answer turneth away wrath: but grievous words
stir up anger. (Proverbs 15:1)

"Mother, I'm thirsty. I'm tired," wailed Lenni.

"Hush, Lenni. We will soon go to the river. There
we will rest and eat some jerky. There you can satisfy
your thirst. The harvest is good today. We must gather
all the berries we can before we return to the village."
Lenni's mother went on picking blackberries with the
other squaws of the Delaware Indian tribe.

Lenni ate a few more berries from his bark basket.
Then he pushed into the thicket of briers again and
reached for the cluster of berries growing there.

Presently the Indians sat on the bank of the
Susquehanna River and shared portions of dried
venison. The water was low. Rocks scattered across the
narrow bed made the water go splashing and swirling
on its way.

"Listen!" Everyone was suddenly still. There was
someone in the forest behind them. But it was not
enemies. Warriors would not make any sounds. This
was the sound of children talking.

Everyone relaxed again. Lenni's sister Munhoka
stole into the woods to see who was there. She returned

to report a group of squaws and children of the Shawnee tribe. They were also gathering berries. Some of the Delaware squaws murmured about this, but a wise old squaw reminded them that there were many more berries than they could gather anyway.

The Shawnees soon discovered them. With sign language the women agreed that all could gather berries together.

The children eyed each other shyly. Munhoka smiled at a little Shawnee girl, and the girl smiled back. Then the girl squatted down and patted the ground with her hand. Lenni squatted, too, and brushed a small spot of ground bare of leaves. Several more Shawnee children gathered around. One of them drew a circle on the bare spot.

There was a small movement in the leaves Lenni had disturbed. A large grasshopper squirmed into sight. Lenni made a grab for it but missed, and the grasshopper sprang into the air. Quick as a flash one of the Shawnee boys captured the grasshopper and held it up for the others to see its squirming legs. Lenni reached for the grasshopper. He had found it first. But the boy drew back with an unkind look and said some angry words Lenni could not understand.

"Mine! Give it!" snapped Lenni, grabbing for the boy's hand. The boy jumped up with more angry words and ran off a little way. Lenni jumped up to chase him, but another Shawnee child grabbed him and made him fall. Lenni's friends then struck at the Shawnee children, and quarreling broke out all around.

The noise attracted the squaws' attention. Each of the children tried to explain to his mother what had happened.

"My grasshopper!"

"She hit me!"

"He started it!"

"He pushed me into the dirt!"

Angry looks spread over the squaws' faces and they turned on one another. With angry shouts and gestures the Delaware squaws drove the Shawnees toward the shallow river.

Making sure they had their children and berries secure, the Shawnees splashed into the water and made their way across. On the far bank, they turned and shouted threats before disappearing into the forest.

Suddenly everyone felt an urge to go home to the protection of their braves. Indignation grew as they rehearsed the incident on the way. "First they take of our harvest. Then they start a war with our papooses. Then they make angry words across the water. I wonder what they said."

"They probably go to call their braves to war."

"Their braves shall not overcome in war. Our braves shall destroy them."

With their grievous words the squaws soon had the Delaware warriors stirred up. They held a counsel and declared war on the Shawnees.

The Shawnee braves likewise were angered by the

report of their squaws. They set out on the warpath
and met the Delaware warriors. A battle followed which
cost many lives and reduced the Shawnee tribe to half
its former number.

Enemies at Peace

When a man's ways please the Lord, he maketh even his
enemies to be at peace with him. (Proverbs 16:7)

"There, Buttercup. Go on, Daisy." Peter directed
the cows into the small log barn, and then he took a
three-legged stool from its peg on the wall.

"Peter! Peter!" Sarah darted into the stall, her face
pale beneath her freckles. Her eyes, usually sparkling,
were wide and anxious. "Peter, Neighbor Blake was
here. He told Father . . ." She caught her breath and
then hurried on. "He told Father the Indians are coming
tonight!"

Peter stared. "The Indians? What did he mean,
Sarah? The Indians are our friends." Peter sat down
and began to milk Daisy.

"Not now—not any more. They are angry. Neighbor
Blake says they are coming to kill all the settlers on
this side of the river!"

Peter's eyes grew round. Just then Father stepped
into the barn. "Father," cried Peter, "you have always
been a friend to the Indians. Remember how you gave
them corn last winter when their food supplies were
low?"

"And Mother has often given food to Indians who

stopped by our house," Sarah added. "They know we are their friends, don't they, Father?"

"I believe they do," Father spoke calmly. "We have tried to show them the love of God. We don't know what the Indians will do," he went on, "but whatever happens, we are safe in God's hands. We do not need to fear."

Twilight was falling as Peter carried a full bucket of foamy milk to the house. Father closed the barn door securely and then picked up the other milk bucket. Sarah hurried along the path, close by Father's side. A screech owl's eerie cry rang from the nearby woods, and Sarah jumped. "Father!"

"It is only an owl, Sarah," Father spoke kindly.

"I know—I know," Sarah quavered. She was trembling when they entered the house, and her face was paler than before.

There was peace in the cozy kitchen. Soft lamplight shone over the simple meal spread on the table. It cast a gentle glow on Mother's serene face. Sarah began to relax. Mother did not seem to be at all worried.

The family did not talk much as they ate their soup and corn bread. It was Peter who broke the silence to ask, "Father, what about the latchstring?"

"What do you mean?"

"I mean—" Peter hesitated. He thought he knew the answer already. "Will you pull the latchstring inside tonight?" His eyes turned toward the door. The latchstring was a leather thong tied to a wooden bar.

Peter swallowed hard. "Why didn't the Indians come here?" he wondered.

"They were here. See this." Father held out several wild turkey feathers and a handful of brightly colored beads. "We found these on the table. The Indians left them here as a sign to us, I believe, to show us that they were here and left peaceably."

Sarah appeared in the doorway, wide-eyed. "You mean the Indians were right here in our house while we were asleep?" her voice rose excitedly.

"Yes, the Indians were here in our house, but the angel of the Lord was here, too," Mother stated simply.

"The latchstring," Peter remembered. "The Indians found the latchstring out! They could see we wanted to be their friends."

"And God moved their hearts to leave us in peace," Father spoke reverently. "Come, let us kneel together and thank Him for His care."

Lesson 24

The Rich Poor

There is that maketh himself rich, yet hath nothing: there
is that maketh himself poor, yet hath great riches. (Proverbs 13:7)

The plains of Iowa where the Hooleys lived were rich
in Indian lore. Arrowheads scattered through their farm
testified to the history of the place. Justin and Arnold
enjoyed searching the ground for arrowheads, and they
each treasured a collection of the relics. Justin had a
much better collection than Arnold, for he was more
diligent about getting and keeping the best for himself.

One spring Saturday their friend Timothy visited
the farm. "What a show!" he exclaimed when he saw
Justin's display of arrowheads. "That collection would
really be worth some money. Where did you get them?"

"They were all picked up on our farm," Justin
answered. "We like to walk through the fields after the
ground has been worked."

"Father was plowing this morning. Would you like
to hunt arrowheads?" suggested Arnold.

The boys sauntered along the furrows with their
eyes on the ground. Arnold spotted a stone point in the
ground and called Timothy. "Can you see the arrowhead
beside my foot?" he asked. "Watch for little corners like
that. They'll be dirty when you find them."

Timothy picked up the stone point and rubbed off the dirt. "This is fun!"

"You may have that one," offered Arnold.

"Thank you," beamed Timothy. "You really found it, though."

The Hooley boys each gathered a handful that day. Timothy had also found one on his own and was eagerly searching for more. "Look at this!" he cried as he dug a stone from the furrow and rubbed the soil from it.

"That's a big one!" exclaimed Arnold, "and it's perfectly whole."

"I believe it's quartz," commented Justin. "It's beautiful." To himself he added, "How grand that would look in my collection! I wonder if Timothy would trade with me."

"I would be glad to trade ten arrowheads for your big one," Justin offered aloud. "Then you would have a dozen pieces in your collection, and I would have something to add to my collection. I haven't found anything today that is worth very much."

Timothy hesitated, rubbing the stone in his hand. "It's such a beauty," he thought. "I don't really care about having a big collection; I like this one. But Justin does seem to want it pretty much."

"All right, I'll trade," he agreed.

At school the next week, Justin mentioned the arrowheads to Timothy. "Are you going to build a display case for your arrowheads?" he asked as they ate their lunch.

"I guess not," Timothy answered.

"We could help you if you don't know how," Justin offered.

"Don't bother, they're not worth displaying," Timothy mumbled, turning away.

One October weekend the brothers enjoyed a visit from a Pennsylvania cousin. Jerry admired their arrowhead collections, especially Justin's. "How do you find them?" he wondered. "I'd like to hunt for some, too."

The boys chose a newly harvested cornfield and each scanned a couple of rows as they walked along. Arnold spied a point of stone and stopped to dig out the whole piece. It proved to be an arrowhead in fair condition. A good while later Jerry pounced on a small, sharp-edged stone. "Is this an arrowhead?" he asked excitedly.

"I think it's a piece of one," Justin confirmed. "It doesn't have a point anymore, but it clearly shows marks of being chipped into a spearhead shape."

No more arrowheads were discovered that afternoon, but the boys did not consider the time wasted. "It was a lovely day to do anything outside," said Justin, "even if we didn't find much."

"I'm glad I found at least one," declared Jerry. "It will be a souvenir of this trip."

"You may have the one I found, too," offered Arnold. "It would be nice to have a little collection of your own." Back in the house Arnold chose a few more pieces from his own collection to add to Jerry's souvenir.

"What a beauty!" exclaimed Jerry as Arnold offered

him a perfect peach-colored point. "But I don't like to take all these nice ones from your collection."

"I can always find more, but you don't have the chance very often," explained Arnold.

A few weeks later a flat package arrived in the mail, addressed to Arnold. "It's from Jerry," he guessed, noting the return address. It *was* from Jerry, and the package yielded a nature book on birds.

"Thank you so much for a wonderful weekend," Jerry wrote. "I want to thank you especially for the arrowheads you gave me. I took them to school because we were studying about Indians. Everybody was interested in them.

"This book is a little gift for you. Come to visit us sometime."

"Did he mean just you?" wondered Justin, picking up the book.

"Oh, I'm sure he'd want you to come, too," declared Arnold.

"Who gave him the arrowheads?" asked Mother, seeing Justin's interest in the book.

"He found one and I gave him some from my collection," explained Arnold.

"Then the book is Arnold's," decided Mother. "Justin has his arrowheads. This is something Arnold has instead of a fine set of arrowheads. And I believe he has a satisfaction, too, that is a special blessing for those who willingly share." She smiled into her son's happy face.

Better Than Great Treasure

Better is little with the fear of the Lord than great treasure
and trouble therewith. (Proverbs 15:16)

The tears ran freely down ten-year-old Julia's cheeks. Seating herself on the swing, she glanced back at the house she had just left. She could still hear Aunt Lorraine loudly scolding Jeffrey for his part in the mischief that had ended in the ruin of her precious chime clock.

"She hardly lets us do anything because she's so afraid we'll scratch or break something," Julia thought bitterly. "It's no wonder Jeffrey gets into so much mischief. We can't please her no matter how hard we try.

"If only Father and Mother hadn't been killed in that terrible accident," her bitter thoughts continued. "Then I wouldn't have to live here with Aunt Lorraine. And I wouldn't have to put up with Jeffrey, either. He can be so mean sometimes."

Ten minutes later Aunt Lorraine called, "Julia, come now if you want dinner."

Julia slowly got up and walked to the house. The family did not sit at the table to eat. Aunt Lorraine would usually fix something for Julia and Jeffrey. Today Julia preferred to be alone. She would take her food out and sit on the swing to eat.

Jeffrey was sitting on a stool near the table, a frightful pout on his face.

"Mother, you knew I didn't want hot dogs for dinner!" he screamed, kicking his feet against the legs of the stool. "I want a hamburger and ice cream for my dinner."

"Not this time, Jeffrey." Julia could tell that Aunt Lorraine was trying to keep the anger out of her own voice.

Julia quickly grabbed her hot dog and escaped to her more peaceful refuge, the swing. Aunt Lorraine had said no to Jeffrey, but Julia knew that in the end Jeffrey would probably win the argument.

That evening Julia was curled on the sofa with a book. Jeffrey was on the floor, surrounded with stuffed animals and toy trucks and tractors. He was playing with his new dump truck, making it go round and round in circles. But by the look on his face, Julia could tell that he really was not interested in his toys.

"Mother," he blurted finally, "I need a new electric train like the one Daryl got for his birthday."

"But Jeffrey, you have so many toys already," Aunt Lorraine protested, motioning in the direction of Jeffrey's scattered disarray.

"I know," Jeffrey answered with a pout, "but these toys are old and I'm tired of them." He gave his teddy bear a toss. It landed on the sofa beside Julia. "Mother, you have to get me an electric train! Promise me,

Mother!" The look in his eyes dared her to go against his wishes.

Aunt Lorraine sighed. "We'll see," she replied. It sounded like an uncommitted answer, but the triumphant look in Jeffrey's eyes showed that he knew he had won again.

"Julia," Aunt Lorraine said one day several weeks later, "I have been checking around about a foster home for you. You will be going to live with the Keller family next week."

Fear shone in Julia's eyes. "Why, Aunt Lorraine?" she asked. "Why can't I stay here with you?"

But Aunt Lorraine did not offer an explanation. The following week a lady from the welfare agency took Julia to her new home on the Keller farm.

It was nearly dinnertime when Julia arrived. So after she had been introduced to the entire Keller family (there surely seemed to be a lot of them, Julia thought), Mother announced that dinner was ready.

Mother put her arm around Julia's trembling shoulders and led her to her place at the table. After setting a big kettle of soup on the table, Mother sat down, too. By this time the rest of the family had all found their places at the table.

After prayer Julia watched as Father dipped soup for each of the children. When her turn came, she held her hand over her bowl. "I don't like soup," she said.

"But you will eat a little anyway," Father said firmly, pulling her bowl out from under her hand. Julia noticed that his voice was not angry like Aunt Lorraine's would have been. It was firm, but very kind. She also noticed that none of the other children complained about the soup. How different these children seemed from her spoiled little cousin!

As Julia ate her soup, she quietly observed her new surroundings. The house was not nearly as pretty as Aunt Lorraine's—and not nearly as new, she was sure. Something seemed to be missing, and at first she did not know what it was. Oh, yes,, the pretty knickknacks—the things that so often got Jeffrey into trouble. Here there were not many extra pretties at all; only a few mottoes on the wall and a jar of colorful flowers in the center of the table.

After dinner Alice Keller, who was about Julia's age, came shyly to Julia and took her hand. "Mother says I must dry the dishes, but she said I could show you our playhouse first while Rebekah starts washing them."

When the girls entered the playhouse, Alice picked up her doll and handed her to Julia. "This is my little Rosie," she said. "Would you like to hold her? Mother made her for me."

Julia looked at Rosie and then at the other dolls that lay in their cribs of cardboard boxes. None of them was as pretty as her own Janie and Kaye. Julia looked at Alice's face. Again she thought of Jeffrey. Alice seemed much happier with these homemade things than Jeffrey did with all his expensive toys.

"Alice, time to dry dishes!" Mother called.

Alice laid Rosie back into her crib. Then she started for the house, and Julia followed.

Julia watched in amazement as Alice cheerfully picked up her dishtowel and joined Rebekah in singing, "With Jesus in the family, it's a happy, happy home; happy, happy home; happy, happy home." She tried to imagine Aunt Lorraine getting her to work like this. Julia knew that if she would have been told to dry the dishes, she would have put up quite a fuss. But these girls were actually singing as they worked!

"How can you be so happy when you have to work and have to eat soup for dinner?" she finally blurted out.

Rebekah turned to her with a smile. "It's Jesus that makes us happy, just like the song says," she explained. "It isn't work or play that makes us happy, or special food either. We are happy when we love Jesus and live the way the Bible teaches. It makes us happy to do something useful to help others."

Julia was quiet. This family was so different from any other family she knew, but she could tell already that she would be happy here.

The Best Medicine

A merry heart doeth good like a medicine: but a broken spirit drieth the bones. (Proverbs 17:22)

A forlorn Betsy huddled on the chair by her mother's bed. Mother had pneumonia. She had started coughing after that rainy day when Baby Joe was so sick. Father did not come home, and they had no telephone. Finally Mother had become so desperate that she walked two miles to Neighbor Coopers. They took her and the baby to the doctor. But Baby Joe had died.

It seemed as though all the light was gone from life. When Father did come home, he was drunk. He brought no comfort to Mother and Betsy. Instead, he became angry and blamed them for Baby Joe's death. Where was Father now? Betsy did not know. It might be a long time before she saw him again. She wasn't sure she even wanted to see him.

Aunt Nora quietly entered the bedroom. "Here you are," she whispered. "Come, Betsy, I have some lunch ready for you."

Betsy sat before her lunch at the table. Aunt Nora had brought some goodies with her, and prepared some tasty soup and a sandwich for Betsy. But Betsy was not hungry. She placed her arms on the table and laid her head down on them.

"Eat something, child," Aunt Nora encouraged. "We don't want you to be sick, too."

Betsy took a small spoonful of soup, but it choked her. "Is Mother going to die?" she asked in a small voice.

"We are praying that God will heal her," answered Aunt Nora. "Perhaps we will need to take her to the hospital so that the doctors can help her better."

Aunt Nora did not tell Betsy about her own concern. Her sister was not responding to the medicine, but rather seemed to be getting worse. "I think you should stay away from Mother's room," she said gently as she filled a cup with broth for Mother. "It tires her to have any commotion near."

Later Aunt Nora began to clean up the kitchen. "I'll soon help you get some of your things together," she told Betsy. "You can go home with me this afternoon."

Betsy stole into her mother's room again. She would be very still, but she wanted to be near Mother. If Mother was going to the hospital, Betsy wanted to be sick and go along. If Mother died, Betsy wanted to die too. Curled up in the armchair, Betsy put her head in her arms and wept.

The door opened and footsteps entered the bedroom. Betsy looked up. Father! A dart of fear shot through her, but immediately it was replaced with wonder. Somehow Father looked different. His face was tender, and there were tears in his eyes.

Father stood by the bed and took Mother's hand. "Elizabeth," he whispered brokenly, "I'm so sorry. I am sorry for all the grief I have caused you. I am sorry for my past rebellion against God. God has forgiven me, Elizabeth, and I am a new man. Oh, I pray that He will give me the opportunity to make a new life for you."

Mother's eyes opened. They brightened. A glad smile spread over her face. "Praise God," she whispered. She squeezed Father's hand and held it a while. Soon she fell asleep with a gentle smile on her face.

Father turned to wide-eyed Betsy. "My child," he said. He held out his arms and Betsy went to him for a hug. They left the bedroom so that they could talk—talk to Aunt Nora, talk about salvation, talk about Mother, talk about household needs.

"I'm hungry," declared Betsy. "Could we have a snack? I feel so good—all bubbly inside. I wouldn't want to be sick now."

When Mother woke from her nap, she wanted to sit up and drink some more broth. Her face was bright and had a healthy color. She did not talk much, but she wanted the others to be in the room and talk to her.

Hospital plans were dropped. Betsy did not go home with Aunt Nora. Father got some directions about Mother's medicine and care. The next day Mother talked and laughed with them. Soon she was able to be out of bed and take part in household activities. "You brought me the best medicine there could be," she told Father joyfully.

Fuel for Fire

Where no wood is, there the fire goeth out: so where there is no talebearer, the strife ceaseth.

As coals are to burning coals, and wood to fire; so is a contentious man to kindle strife.

The words of a talebearer are as wounds, and they go down into the innermost parts of the belly. (Proverbs 26:20–22)

Mr. Ford and Mr. Mackenzie wanted to help their neighbor, Widow Spencer. They agreed together to cut her winter firewood. But the two busy men could not seem to find a time that suited them both. Several times one or the other proposed a woodcutting. Once when Mr. Ford suggested it, Mr. Mackenzie needed to help his brother's family to move. When Mr. Mackenzie wanted to spend a day cutting wood, Mr. Ford was called for emergency service on his job. Another time he was sick with flu.

One day Mr. Ford mentioned the project when he was talking with another neighbor, Mr. Strife. "I suppose I'll have to just go after some wood myself one of these days. I wouldn't want Mrs. Spencer to fret about a low supply when winter sets in."

Mr. Strife approached Mr. Mackenzie and reported, "Roger Ford is disgusted with you for not helping to cut

Mrs. Spencer's wood. He said he'll probably have to do all the work himself."

"Well, he needn't get irritated about it," retorted Sam Mackenzie. "I tried more often than he did to get at it together. But I'm not interested in working with him if he wants to quarrel about it."

Mr. Strife returned to Mr. Ford with this piece of kindling. "Sam Mackenzie is really hot under the collar. He said he's not going to help you with any woodcutting."

"Well, if he's so hot, he doesn't need much firewood," fumed Mr. Ford. "I'll just help myself to part of his wood to stack his share of Mrs. Spencer's pile. He doesn't break his promise that easily."

Soon Mr. Strife was back at Mr. Mackenzie's door. "Roger's going to steal your whole woodpile," he warned. "He's mad as a hornet."

"Let him come," scorned Sam. "While he's loading up my wood, I'll go make firewood out of his house. He has more firewood than he knows."

Mr. Strife sounded the alarm. "Roger, Sam's going to burn down your house! You ought to have him arrested."

But Mr. Strife himself was arrested that night. His character had led him into dishonest business, and he was finally caught in his sin. He was imprisoned for a short term and had no opportunity to visit Mr. Ford and Mr. Mackenzie.

Without his reports to stir them up, the two men

290

turned to more worthwhile thoughts about Mrs. Spencer's woodpile. One frosty Saturday they chanced to meet in the Spencer wood lot.

"What brings you out this morning?" asked Mr. Ford cautiously.

"The same thing you're here for," guessed Mr. Mackenzie, searching Roger's face.

"You don't care if we work together?"

"I'd rather. You don't object?"

"We'll get more done. I don't have anything against you."

"I'm not angry either. What was the whole fuss about anyway?"

"I think it was all just Strife," decided Mr. Ford.

The woods rang with a hearty laugh and the song of the saws.

Thou Shalt Understand

Yea, if thou criest after knowledge, and liftest up thy voice for understanding;

If thou seekest her as silver, and searchest for her as for hid treasures;

Then shalt thou understand the fear of the Lord, and find the knowledge of God. (Proverbs 2:3–5)

John Bunyan wiped the letters from his slate and put it and the slate pencil up on the mantel. There would be no more school for him. John had barely mastered the skills of reading and writing. But the family was poor, and John's work was needed to help provide their food.

Father was a tinker. He had taught John how to mend pots and pans. As John worked with Father, he also learned how to make new utensils. He traveled with Father about Bedford, England, serving many customers and learning the trade of a tinker.

But John Bunyan also learned many sinful habits. The Bunyans were not Christian people, and no one taught John about God. He lied and cheated. He was disrespectful to his parents. When he was sixteen, the unhappy boy left home and joined the army.

A few years later John was married, and he settled down in Bedford to work as a tinker. His wife had some

Bible knowledge and she often talked to him about God. She encouraged him to study. She helped him to read some books her father had given them.

John tried very hard to stop sinning. He stopped swearing and cheating. He went to church regularly. He thought this was the way to please God. One day as John was peddling his pots and pans, he met some Christians who told him about the blood of Jesus. They told him that simply changing his ways would not save him.

John began to read the Bible. He looked for other chances to talk to the Christians he had met. He had many questions. These friends sent him to a minister who could help him to understand what he read. The more John read his Bible, the more he wanted to talk about it. He soon realized that he was a great sinner. The good things he tried to do would not save him.

"How wicked I have been!" he cried. "Can God forgive all the sins I have committed?" He prayed much for God to have mercy on him. The desire to know God and have peace with him became the most important thing in his life. Then John became sick. How discouraged he was! He could only think of his sins. While he was sick, he read a book that helped him to understand salvation. He believed in the Lord and was saved.

From that time on, John's life was changed. Now as he went from house to house, he told the people about the Lord Jesus Christ. His tinker business grew. He told many people about salvation through Jesus' blood.

At that time England had a law against anyone except ordained ministers preaching. So John's preaching soon got him into trouble with the authorities. He was arrested and sentenced to three months in prison.

The judge wanted John to promise that he would no longer preach. John refused to make the promise, so he was not released after three months. His imprisonment dragged on for twelve years! But John did not waste those twelve years. He told the other prisoners about the Lord. He worshiped and prayed with them, and he also made use of this time to do some writing.

When John Bunyan was released, he went right on telling others about the Lord. He became the pastor of a church, but he was still threatened about his preaching. A few years later he was put into prison again. While there, he continued his writing. One of the results of his work is the book *Pilgrim's Progress*, which has been loved and studied for hundreds of years. This book shows that John Bunyan came to understand very well the fear and the knowledge of the Lord.

No Lack

He that giveth unto the poor shall not lack: but he that hideth his eyes shall have many a curse. (Proverbs 28:27)

He that hath pity upon the poor lendeth unto the Lord; and that which he hath given will he pay him again. (Proverbs 19:17)

As a young minister in Bristol, England, George Mueller was burdened for the needy children in the city. Orphans who had no one to care for them were kept at the poorhouse with the insane and aged. The children were like prisoners living there until they were old enough to be somebody's servants. They did not even receive an education.

George prayed about the need. He wanted to start an orphanage, but he had no money. Plans began to grow in his mind. He would rent a large house and take in twenty or thirty orphans. He would provide for them and educate them as his own children.

But the money! George had often encouraged poor people to trust in God for their needs. Now he decided that he would need to do the same. He would simply pray for the money and the supplies, and he would never ask any person to give money for the orphanage.

As soon as people heard that George planned to start an orphanage, they started giving gifts. Almost faster than he could receive them came dishes, furniture, and clothes, pennies, shillings, and pounds—along with helpers for the household.

A few months later George and Mary Mueller had forty-two orphans in their care. But there were many more children needing help. Within a year George opened a place for homeless babies. The next year he rented a third house, which was immediately filled with orphan boys. Things went well the first two years. People gave enough to support all three homes.

But times of testing came. One day George prayed, "Lord, they need ten pounds today at the Infants' Home. I gave them everything in the treasury, but that was only five pounds. They need five pounds more. I am trusting You to supply it somehow."

A few minutes later a woman stopped in. "The Lord told me I should not wear these gaudy jewels any more. And I felt He wanted me to sell them and give the money to someone else. I thought of the orphans," she said, laying a handful of coins on George's desk. Her donation amounted to five pounds and a few shillings.

The workers cheerfully gave everything they could to help provide. But there came a day when they had nothing more to give, and money was needed for food. "Should we sell some furnishings or other things that could be spared?" they wondered. George prayed that the Lord might send help so that this would not be necessary.

Then a visitor from London came to see him. She had

been next door to the Boys' House five days, and now she was finally bringing the gift of money that had been sent with her for the orphans.

Day by day the Muellers and their helpers prayed for the things they needed. It was unusual to have enough on hand to feed the children three days ahead. But the food was always there when they needed it. The orphans never went hungry, and they never suffered for want of clothes.

One winter there was trouble with the heating system of a large orphan house. George was concerned that the children, especially the little ones, should not suffer from being in cold rooms. He would need to let the fire go out while the repair work was being done, which could take several days. A cold north wind had brought the first really cold weather of the winter, but the repairs could not be delayed any longer. George prayed that they might have a south wind and that the workers would be eager to finish the job as soon as possible.

When the day came to let the fire die, there was a change in the weather. A pleasant south wind made it so warm that a fire was unnecessary. In the evening the manager of the workers told his men to work late and start again early in the morning. "We would rather work all night," his workers responded. They finished the repairs that night, and by morning the boiler was ready for fire again. All that time the weather was so warm that no one suffered from cold.

The work prospered and grew. The time came when

the orphans no longer lived in rented houses in the city, for enough money had been donated to build five large houses. They stood on the hills of Ashley Down along the river north of Bristol.

God was always faithful in providing for George Mueller's orphanages. Not only did they have enough money to supply their own needs, but they were able to support mission work as well.

Diligent in His Business

Seest thou a man diligent in his business? he shall stand before kings; he shall not stand before mean men. (Proverbs 22:29)

The purple shadows of evening darkened the large Virginia plantation as a little dark-skinned boy ran down the path to the slave cabins. He had been sent on an errand to the big plantation house, and he was glad to hurry back to the warm cabin. His mother looked up with a smile as he entered. "That's a good boy, Booker. Back in a hurry."

Booker Washington stretched out before the fireplace. His dark eyes became dreamy as he watched the flames leap above the hickory logs. "Mother," he began in a soft, slow voice. "Mother, what do you think I saw this morning?"

"I don't know, child."

"When I carried the books for the master's children, I looked inside the schoolhouse. I saw it, Mother!" His voice rose excitedly. "I saw inside the schoolhouse!"

"Inside the schoolhouse!" His mother sounded astonished.

"What did it look like?" his brother John asked curiously.

"It looked good." Booker's eyes shone at the memory. "Boys and girls were sitting on benches. All of them were holding books in their hands. I wish I had a book."

"What would you do with a book?"

"I'd learn to read it. I've made up my mind—I'm going to learn to read," Booker stated firmly.

"How could you learn to read, Booker?" Mother asked gently. "You can't go to school. None of our people can read."

"I know, Mother. But I want to learn to read. Someday I will find a way."

When Booker was nine years old, all the black slaves were set free. They could leave their masters and go to live wherever they wished. Booker's stepfather found work in a salt furnace in West Virginia. Booker worked at the salt furnace with his stepfather. He worked eleven hours a day, packing barrels with salt. This was hard work for a nine-year-old boy. But Booker learned quickly and did his best. The furnace boss was pleased with him.

When a school for black children was opened nearby, Booker was excited. "At last I will learn to read!" To be allowed to go to school, Booker started work at four o'clock in the morning. He worked at the salt furnace until nine and then walked to school. When the school day was over, he went back to the salt furnace and worked from four to six.

Booker worked as diligently in school as he did at the salt furnace. His dream was coming true! He was learning to read. But soon his stepfather took him out of school. "No more school," he ordered. "Booker, you will have to go back to work full time." Booker obeyed his stepfather, but he kept on studying as well as he could. He attended some classes at a night school in the nearby town.

When Booker was twelve, his stepfather put him to work in a coal mine. The work was dangerous, but Booker kept that job for two years. Then he heard about another job.

"Mother, the mine boss's wife needs a boy to work for her," Booker announced. "Do you think I could do that?"

"I believe you could. Would you like to try?"

"Some of the other boys have worked for her. They say Mrs. Ruffner is too strict. George says she expects the yard to be kept perfectly clean. She won't allow even a scrap of paper lying around! Henry said she asked him to paint the fence when it didn't need it. Joe says she is the most particular woman he ever saw. I want to get out of the coal mine, but I don't know if I can please Mrs. Ruffner." Booker's dark face was troubled.

"I think you can, if you are diligent," his mother assured him.

At first Booker was afraid of Mrs. Ruffner, but he soon learned that she was kind as well as particular.

"I expect everything about the yard and house to be kept clean and neat," she instructed Booker. "Never leave trash lying around. When you see a board loose on the fence, repair it immediately. When I send you on an errand, do it promptly. Do you understand?"

"Yes, Ma'am," Booker answered shyly. "I'll do my best, Ma'am." And he did. He kept the grass cut neatly. He kept the fence in good repair and painted it without being told. He became as particular about trash as Mrs. Ruffner herself. He could not bear to see any litter in the yard.

Booker carefully saved all the money he could. He still dreamed of continuing his studies. By the time he was sixteen, Booker had managed to save fifteen dollars. His parents gave their consent, and Booker started out for Hampton Institute five hundred miles away. First he traveled by stagecoach. When his money was used up, he started walking. He begged rides in wagons. Then he worked for a time to earn money for the rest of the trip. At last he arrived.

The head teacher at Hampton Institute looked carefully at the young black boy who stood before her. "You want to be admitted as a student?" she asked doubtfully.

"Yes, Ma'am." Booker's face shone eagerly. But he looked very thin and poor. His clothes were shabby.

What kind of student would he be? The head teacher decided to give him a test. "Here is a classroom that needs to be swept." She showed him the room and said, "Take the broom and sweep it."

Booker knew how to sweep. Mrs. Ruffner had taught him to sweep thoroughly. Eagerly he began. He swept the classroom three times. He moved every piece of furniture. Then he found a dust cloth and dusted the whole room four times. He dusted every bench, table, and desk. He dusted all the woodwork around the walls. He cleaned every closet and every corner.

When Booker was finished, the head teacher came to inspect the classroom. She examined the floor. She peered into the closets. She took her white handkerchief and rubbed it on the woodwork. She rubbed it over the table and desks. Booker watched in breathless silence. Would he pass the test?

At last the teacher turned to him. "I believe you will be a good student, Booker T. Washington. You may begin now as a student at Hampton Institute."

What joy filled Booker's heart! He began studying books as diligently as he had cleaned the classroom.

When Booker was through school, he began teaching at Hampton Institute. By the time he was twenty-five years old, he started a new school especially for blacks. He wanted to help his people to learn many kinds of skills.

Booker became known and respected far beyond the school. Presidents and other government leaders often sought his advice when working on problems between blacks and whites. Booker T. Washington had been a diligent little slave in his boyhood, but now he was a well-known leader of men.

Pronunciation Symbols
Used in the Glossary

/ā/   as in pay
/ē/   as in see
/ī/   as in by
/ō/   as in go
/ū/   as in cube
/o͞o/ as in food

/a/   as in hat
/e/   as in yes
/i/   as in sit
/o/   as in top
/u/   as in bug
/oo/ as in foot

/ou/ as in out
/oi/ as in boy
/ô/   as in saw
/ä/   as in park
/ė/   as in her
/ə/   the indefinite vowel
      sound heard in an
      unaccented syllable,
      representing any of
      the five vowels, as in
      alone, listen, flexible,
      consider, suppose

/sh/ as in she
/ch/ as in chop
/wh/ as in when
/th/ as in thin
/th/ as in that
/ng/ as in sing
/zh/ as in measure

Glossary

Abraham (ā' bra•ham) The father of the Jewish nation

Achaia (a•kā' yə) A peninsula country that extends into the Mediterranean Sea, called Greece today

Adramyttium (a•dra•mit' ē•um) A seaport of Mysia

Adriatic Sea (ā•drē•at' ik) The northern gulf in the Mediterranean Sea

Aeneas (ē•nē' əs) A man of Lydda who was sick with palsy

Agabus (ag' a•bus) A prophet from Jerusalem

Agrippa (a•grip' ə) The name of two Herods who ruled in Palestine

Alexander (al•ig•zan' dər) **1.** A leader at Jerusalem in the council that examined Peter and John **2.** A Jew who tried to address the mob in the theater at Ephesus

Alexandria (al•ig•zan' drē•ə) A seaport city of Egypt known for its library and schools

Alphaeus (al•fē' us) The father of a disciples named James

Alps (alps) A large mountain range in Europe

Amphipolis (am•fip' ō•lis) A city of Macedonia between Philippi and Thessalonica

Ananias (an•a•nī' əs) **1.** A disciple in the early church at Jerusalem **2.** A disciple at Damascus **3.** A high priest before whom Paul was examined

A

Andrew (an' droo) Simon Peter's brother and one of the twelve apostles

Annas (an' əs) A high priest at Jerusalem

Antioch (an' tē•ok) **1.** A city of Syria **2.** A city of Pisidia in Asia Minor

Antipatris (an•tip' a•tris) A town between Jerusalem and Caesarea

Apollonia (ap•o•lō' nē•ə) A city of Macedonia, east of Thessalonica

Apollos (a•pol' əs) An educated Jew from Alexandria

Appii Forum (ap' ē•ī fôr' um) A town in Italy southeast of Rome

Aquila (ak' wil•ə) A Jewish man Paul met at Corinth

Arcturus (ärk•toor' əs) A very bright star in a kite-shaped constellation

Arimathaea (a•ri•ma•thē' ə) The town of the man named Joseph who buried the body of Jesus

Aristarchus (är•is•tär' kus) A Macedonian who travelled with Paul

Asia (ā' zhə) **1.** The largest continent of the world **2.** In Bible times, the land in the western part of Asia Minor

Assos (as' əs) A seaport town near Troas in Mysia

Athens (ath' ənz) The capital city of Greece

Attalia (at•a•lī' ə) A city on the seacoast of Pamphylia

306

Augustus (ä•gus' tus) The Caesar who ruled in Rome at the time Jesus was born

Azotus (a•zō' tus) A Philistine city where Philip preached the Gospel

Barabbas (bär•ab' əs) A Jewish prisoner who was released at the Passover when Jesus was crucified

Bar-jesus (bär•jē' zus) A Jewish sorcerer, also called Elymas

Barnabas (bär' na•bəs) A disciple from Cyprus who traveled with Paul

Barsabas (bär' sə•bəs) The second name of the Joseph who was in the lot to replace Judas as an apostle

Bartholomew (bär•thol' o•mū) One of the twelve apostles, also called Nathanael

Berea (be•rē' ə) An inland city of Macedonia, about fifty miles west of Thessalonica

Bernice (bər•nī' sē) The sister of Agrippa

Bethany (beth' a•nē) A village on the Mount of Olives along the road from Jerusalem to Jericho

Bethlehem (beth' le•hem) A town in the hill country of Judah; the birthplace of David and Jesus

Bethsaida (beth•sā' i•də) A city near the Sea of Galilee

Bildad (bil' dad) A friend who came to visit Job

Bithynia (bī•thin' ē•ə) A province on the northwest coast of Asia Minor, next to Mysia

Caesar (sē' zər) The title of the Roman emperors

Caesarea (ses' a•rē' ə) A city on the coast of Palestine

Caiaphas (kā' a•fəs) The Jewish high priest at the time of Jesus' death

Cana (kā' nə) A city in Galilee

Candace (kan' da•sē) A queen of Ethiopia

Capernaum (ka•pėr' nē•um) A city on the shore of the Sea of Galilee

Cenchrea (sen' krē•ə) A seaport of Greece near Corinth

Cephas (sē' fəs) The name Jesus gave to Simon Peter

Chaldeans (kal•dē' ənz) People from the land of Chaldea, near Mesopotamia and east of Uz

Chios (kī' əs) An island in the Aegean Sea

Cilicia (si•lish' ē•ə) A province of southeast Asia Minor

Clauda (klô' də) A small island off the southwest coast of Crete

Claudius (klô' di•us) The Roman Caesar during the time of Acts

Claudius Lysias (klô' di•us lis' ē•əs) The chief captain over the soldiers at Jerusalem

Cleophas (klē ō•fəs) The husband of Mary who believed in Jesus

Cnidus (nī' dus) A coast city near the island of Coos

Coos (kō' os) An island off the southwest coast of Asia Minor

Corinth (kôr' inth) A city of Greece

Cornelius (kôr•nē' lē•us) A centurion who worshiped God

Crete (krēt) A large island in the Mediterranean Sea, southeast of Greece

Crispus (kris' pus) The ruler of the Jewish synagogue at Corinth

Cyprus (sī' prus) An island in the northeastern part of the Mediterranean Sea

Damascus (da•mas' kus) A chief city of Syria

Delaware (del' ə•wer) An Indian tribe that lived in the eastern United States

Demetrius (dē•mē' tri•us) A silversmith at Ephesus

Derbe (der' bē) A city in the southeastern part of Lycaonia

Diana (dī•an' ə) A Roman goddess

Dorcas (dôr' kəs) A Christian woman of Joppa

Drusilla (droo•sil' ə) The Jewish wife of Felix

Elihu (ē•lī' hū) One of Job's friends

Eliphaz (el' i•faz) A friend who came to visit Job

Elymas (el' ē•məs) A Jewish sorcerer

Ephesus (ef' e•sus) A city on the west coast of Asia Minor

Ephraim (ē frā•im) One of the tribes of Israel, named for Joseph's second son

Erastus (ē•ras' tus) One of the Christians who helped Paul

Ethiopia (ē•thē•ō' pē•ə) A country in Africa southeast of Egypt

Eutychus (ū' tē•kus) A young man of Troas who fell out of a window while sleeping

Fair Havens (fār hā' vənz) A harbor of Crete, near the city of Lasea

Felix (fē' liks) A Roman ruler in the province of Judea

Festus (fes' tus) The Roman ruler in Judea after Felix

Gaius (gā' us) A Macedonian who was with Paul in the uproar at Ephesus

Galatia (ga•lā' shē•ə) A province of central Asia Minor

Galilean (gal•i•lē' ən) Someone from the land of Galilee

Galilee (gal' i•lē) The northern part of Palestine

Gamaliel (ga•mā' lē•əl) A Pharisee of the Jewish Sanhedrin and a teacher of the Law

Gaza (gā' zə) A desert town in southeastern Palestine

Gentile (jen' tīl) Someone who is not a Jew

Greece (grēs) Achaia; a peninsula country that extends into the Mediterranean Sea

Haran (hā' rən) A city of Mesopotamia

Herod (her' əd) The family name of some Roman Rulers in Palestine

Iconium (ī•kō' nē•um) A city in the district of Lycaonia in Asia Minor

Iowa (ī ō•wə) A state in the central part of the United States

Isaiah (ī•zā' ə)   **1.** An Old Testament prophet who prophesied much about Jesus **2.** The book written by this prophet

Iscariot (is•kar' i•ot) The last name of Judas, the disciple who betrayed Jesus

Italian (i•tal' yən) Of Italy, its people, or its customs

Italy (it' ə•lē) The country on the boot-shaped peninsula in the northern part of the Mediterranean Sea

Jason (jā' sən) A Christian at Thessalonica

Jerusalem (je•rōō' sa•ləm) The capital city of Palestine, and religious center for the Jews

Job (jōb) A man from the land of Uz who suffered many trials

Joel (jō əl) An Old Testament prophet who foretold the outpouring of the Holy Spirit

Joppa (jop' ə) A town on the coast of Palestine

Judas (jōo' dəs)   **1.** The apostle who betrayed Jesus **2.** Another apostle, also called Thaddaeus **3.** A man of Galilee who led an unsuccessful revolt

Judea (jōo•dē' ə) The southern part of Palestine

Julius (jōo' lē•us) A centurion of Augustus' band

Jupiter (jōo' pi•tər) The chief god of the Romans

Justus (jus' tus)   **1.** One of the two named in the lot to replace Judas as an apostle **2.** A disciple at Corinth

Kidron (kid' rən) A brook between the Mount of Olives and Jerusalem

Lasea (la•sē' ə) A city on the island of Crete

Lazarus (laz' a•rus) The brother of Mary and Martha of Bethany

Lenni (len' i) An Indian boy

Lucerne (lōo•sėrn') The name of a lake and of a city in Switzerland

Lycaonia (lik•a•ō' nē•ə) An inland district of Asia Minor

Lycia (lish' ē•ə) A province on the south coast of Asia Minor

Lydda (lid' ə) A village about ten miles inland from Joppa

Lydia (lid' ē•ə) A Christian woman in Philippi

Lysias (lis ē•əs) See *Claudius Lysias*

Lystra (lis' trə) A city of Lycaonia, south of Iconium

Macedonia (mas' e•dō nē•ə) The country north of Greece

Magdalene (mag' da•lēn) The second name of a woman named Mary who followed Jesus

Malchus (mal' kus) A servant of the high priest, whose ear Peter cut off

Mars' Hill (märz hil) The hill near Athens where the Romans held court

Matthias (ma•thī' əs) The man who was chosen to be an apostle in the place of Judas

Mazzaroth (maz' ə•roth) Groups of stars that seem to be near the sun at different seasons of the year

Mediterranean (med' i•tə•rā' nē•ən) The large body of water west of Palestine, also called the Great Sea

Melita (mel' i•tə) A small island near Sicily in the Mediterranean Sea

Mercury (mėr' kū•rē) A god of the Romans

Mesopotamia (mes•ō•pō•tā' mē•ə) The land between the Euphrates and Tigris Rivers, northeast of Palestine

Messiah (me•sī' ə) The promised deliverer that was prophesied in the Old Testament; Jesus

Midian (mid' ē•ən) Part of the Arabian desert southeast of Palestine

Miletus (mī•lē' tus) A seaport of Asia Minor about thirty-six miles south of Ephesus

Mitylene (mit' ə•lē' nē) A city on the island of Lesbos

Mnason (nā' sən) A disciple from Cyprus

Mueller (mū' lər), **George** A man of England in the 1800's who built large orphanages

Munhoka (mun•hō' kə) An Indian girl

Myra (mī' rə) A seaport of Lycia

Mysia (mis' ē ə) A province in northwest Asia Minor

Nathanael (na•than' i•əl) A man of Cana who followed Jesus

Nazareth (naz' a•reth) The town in Galilee where Jesus grew up

Neapolis (nē•ap' o•lis) A seaport town of Macedonia

Nero (nē' rō) The Roman emperor after Claudius

Nicanor (ni•kā' nôr) One of the seven deacons ordained in the early church

Nicodemus (nik•ō•dē' mus) A Pharisee who was interested in Jesus' teachings

Nicolas (nik' o•ləs) One of the seven deacons ordained in the early church

Orion (ō•rī' ən) A group of stars that suggests a picture of a man wearing a belt and sword and holding a shield and club

Palestine (pal' is•tīn) The land that was called Canaan in the Old Testament

Pamphylia (pam•fil' ē•ə) A small section on the south coast of Asia Minor

Paphos (pā' fos) A town on the southwest part of Cyprus

Parmenas (pär' me•nəs) One of the seven deacons ordained in the early church

Patara (pat' a•rə) A seaport of Lycia

Pennsylvania (pen•səl•vān' yə) A state in the eastern part of the United States

Pentecost (pen' te•kost) A Jewish feast fifty days after the Passover, at which the Holy Spirit was given

Perga (pėr' gə) A town of Pamphylia

Pharisee (far' i•sē) A member of a high-ranking group among the Jews

Phenice (fē' nis) A harbor city of Crete

Philip (fil' ip) **1.** One of the twelve apostles **2.** One of the seven deacons ordained in the early church

Philippi (fi•lip' ī) A city of Macedonia about nine miles inland from Neapolis

Phoenicia (fe•nish' ē•ə) The coast land along the Mediterranean Sea north of Palestine

Phrygia (frij' ē•ə) A large province of Asia Minor

Pilate (pī' lət) The Roman governor in Judea when Jesus was crucified

Pisidia (pi•sid' ē•ə) A district of Asia Minor next to Pamphylia

Pleiades (plē' ə•dēz) A cluster of stars, six of which can be seen by ordinary sight

Pontus (pon' tus) A province along the north coast of Asia Minor

Priscilla (pri•sil' ə) The wife of Aquila

Prochorus (prok' o•rus) One of the seven deacons ordained in the early church

Ptolemais (tol•e•mā' is) A city on the coast of Palestine

Publius (pub' lē•us) The chief man on the island of Melita

Puteoli (pū•tē' ō•lē) A seaport of Italy

Rhegium (rē' jē•um) A city at the tip of Italy

Rhoda (rō də) A girl at Mary's house where the church was praying for Peter

Rhodes (rōdz) An island off the southest coast of Asia Minor

Rome (rōm) The capital city of Italy

Sabeans (sa•bē ənz) People from a land to the south of Uz

Sadducee (sad' ū•sē) A member of a high-ranking group among the Jews

Salmone (sal•mō' nē) The point of land on the east end of Crete

Samaria (sa•mār' i•ə) The name of the land between Judea and Galilee; also a city in that land

Samaritan (sa•mar' i•tən) A person who lived in Samaria

Samos (sā məs) An island off the coast of Asia Minor, near Ephesus and Miletus

Samothracia (sam•ō•thrā' shē•ə) A small island in the northeastern part of the Aegean Sea

Sapphira (sa•fī' rə) The wife of Ananias who was struck dead

Saron (sā' rən) The fertile seacoast between Joppa and Mt. Carmel

Sceva (sē' və) A chief priest among the Jews

Secundus (sē•kun' dus) A Thessalonian who traveled with Paul

S

Seleucia (sē•loō' shē•ə) A city on the seacoast near Antioch in Syria

Sergius Paulus (sėr' jē•us pôl' us) A deputy of Cyprus

Shawnee (shô•nē') A tribe of Indians who lived in the forests of North America

Sidon (sī' dən) A city on the coast of Phoenicia

Silas (sī' ləs) A disciple who traveled with the Apostle Paul

Siloam (sī•lō' əm) A pool at Jerusalem

Simon Peter (sī' mən pē' tər) Andrew's brother and one of the twelve apostles

Solomon (sol' o•mən) The richest and wisest king of Israel

Sopater (sō' pa•tər) A Christian at Berea

Sosthenes (sos' thə•nēz) A ruler of the Jewish synagogue at Corinth

Stephen (stē' fən) One of the seven deacons ordained in the early church

Susquehanna (sus•kwe•han' ə) A river in the eastern part of the United States

Sychar (sī' kär) A town in Samaria at Jacob's well

Syracuse (sir' a•kūs) A city on the east coast of Sicily

Syria (sir' ē•ə) The country north of Palestine along the Mediterranean Sea

Tarsus (tär' sus) The chief city of Cilicia

Tertullus (tər•tul' us) An orator hired by the Jews to speak at Paul's trial

Thessalonica (thes•a•lo•nī' kə) An important city in Macedonia

Theudas (thoo' dəs) A man who led an unsuccessful group of about four hundred

Three Taverns (thrē tav' ərnz) A small town in Italy, near Appii Forum

Thyatira (thī•a•tī' rə) A city in Asia Minor

Tiberius (tī•bē' ri•us) The Roman Ceasar after Augustus

Timon (tī mən) One of the seven deacons ordained in the early church

Timothy (tim' ō•thē) A disciple from Lystra who accompanied Paul in his journeys

Troas (trō' əs) A seaport of Mysia in Asia Minor

Trogyllium (trō•jil' ē•um) The point of land and a town across a narrow channel from the island of Samos

Trophimus (trof' i•mus) A Gentile Christian of Ephesus

Tychicus (tik' i•kus) A Christian of Asia Minor

Tyrannus (tī•ran' us) A man of Ephesus who let Paul teach at his school

Tyre (tīr) A seacoast city of Phoenicia

U–Z

Uz (uz) A land of the Middle East between Damascus and Edom

Zacharias (zak•a•rī' əs) A priest at the time of Jesus' birth; the father of John the Baptist

Zebedee (zeb' e•dē) A fisherman of Galilee; the father of the disciples James and John

Zechariah (zek•a•rī' ə) **1.** An Old Testament prophet who told of Jesus' coming **2.** The book written by this prophet

Zelotes (zē•lō' tēz) The second name of an apostle named Simon

Zophar (zō' fər) A friend who came to visit Job

- Rome
- Three Taverns
- Appii Forum

Puteoli

ITALY

Adriatic Sea

Philippi •
Amphipolis •
Thessalonica
Berea •

• Neap
• Apollonia

SAM
THR

MACEDONIA

Aegean Sea

• Rhegium

SICILY

• Syracuse

ᘒ MELITA

Corinth •
Cenchrea •
GREECE

• Athens
•

CRE

CLAUDA ᘒ Fair